THE TEACHING FOR SOCIAL JUSTICE SERIES
William Ayers—*Series Editor*
Therese Quinn—*Associate Series Editor*

Editorial Board: Hal Adams, Barbara Bowman, Lisa Delpit, Michelle Fine, Maxine Greene,
Caroline Heller, Annette Henry, Asa Hilliard, Rashid Khalidi, Gloria Ladson-Billings, Charles Payne,
Mark Perry, Luis Rodriguez, Jonathan Silin, William Watkins

Deep Knowledge:
Learning to Teach Science for Understanding and Equity
DOUGLAS B. LARKIN

Bad Teacher! How Blaming Teachers
Distorts the Bigger Picture
KEVIN K. KUMASHIRO

Crossing Boundaries—
Teaching and Learning with Urban Youth
VALERIE KINLOCH

The Assault on Public Education: Confronting the Politics
of Corporate School Reform
WILLIAM H. WATKINS, EDITOR

Pedagogy of the Poor:
Building the Movement to End Poverty
WILLIE BAPTIST & JAN REHMANN

Grow Your Own Teachers:
Grassroots Change for Teacher Education
ELIZABETH A. SKINNER, MARIA TERESA GARRETÓN, & BRIAN D.
SCHULTZ, EDITORS

Girl Time:
Literacy, Justice, and the School-to-Prison Pipeline
MAISHA T. WINN

Holler If You Hear Me: The Education of a Teacher and His
Students, Second Edition
GREGORY MICHIE

Controversies in the Classroom:
A Radical Teacher Reader
JOSEPH ENTIN, ROBERT C. ROSEN, & LEONARD VOGT, EDITORS

Spectacular Things Happen Along the Way:
Lessons from an Urban Classroom
BRIAN D. SCHULTZ

The Seduction of Common Sense: How the Right Has
Framed the Debate on America's Schools
KEVIN K. KUMASHIRO

Teach Freedom:
Education for Liberation in the African-American Tradition
CHARLES M. PAYNE & CAROL SILLS STRICKLAND, EDITORS

Social Studies for Social Justice:
Teaching Strategies for the Elementary Classroom
RAHIMA C. WADE

Pledging Allegiance:
The Politics of Patriotism in America's Schools
JOEL WESTHEIMER, EDITOR

See You When We Get There:
Teaching for Change in Urban Schools
GREGORY MICHIE

Echoes of Brown:
Youth Documenting and Performing the Legacy
of *Brown v. Board of Education*
MICHELLE FINE

Writing in the Asylum:
Student Poets in City Schools
JENNIFER MCCORMICK

Teaching the Personal and the Political:
Essays on Hope and Justice
WILLIAM AYERS

Teaching Science for Social Justice
ANGELA CALABRESE BARTON, WITH JASON L. ERMER, TANAHIA A.
BURKETT, & MARGERY D. OSBORNE

Putting the Children First:
The Changing Face of Newark's Public Schools
JONATHAN G. SILIN & CAROL LIPPMAN, EDITORS

Refusing Racism:
White Allies and the Struggle for Civil Rights
CYNTHIA STOKES BROWN

A School of Our Own: Parents, Power, and Community at
the East Harlem Block Schools
TOM RODERICK

The White Architects of Black Education:
Ideology and Power in America, 1865–1954
WILLIAM WATKINS

The Public Assault on America's Children:
Poverty, Violence, and Juvenile Injustice
VALERIE POLAKOW, EDITOR

Construction Sites: Excavating Race, Class, and Gender
Among Urban Youths
LOIS WEIS & MICHELLE FINE, EDITORS

Walking the Color Line:
The Art and Practice of Anti-Racist Teaching
MARK PERRY

A Simple Justice:
The Challenge of Small Schools
WILLIAM AYERS, MICHAEL KLONSKY, &
GABRIELLE H. LYON, EDITORS

Teaching for Social Justice:
A Democracy and Education Reader
WILLIAM AYERS, JEAN ANN HUNT, & THERESE QUINN

EDUCATION LIBRARY
UNIVERSITY OF KENTUCKY

Deep Knowledge

Learning to Teach Science for Understanding and Equity

Douglas B. Larkin

Foreword by Gloria Ladson-Billings

Teachers College, Columbia University
New York and London

Educ.
Q
181
.L37
2013

Published by Teachers College Press, 1234 Amsterdam Avenue, New York, NY 10027

Copyright © 2013 by Teachers College, Columbia University

All rights reserved. No part of this publication may be reproduced or transmitted in any form or by any means, electronic or mechanical, including photocopy, or any information storage and retrieval system, without permission from the publisher.

Library of Congress Cataloging-in-Publication Data

Larkin, Douglas B.
Deep knowledge : learning to teach science for understanding and equity / Douglas B. Larkin.
   pages cm
Includes bibliographical references and index.
ISBN 978-0-8077-5421-4 (pbk. : alk. paper)
ISBN 978-0-8077-5422-1 (hardcover : alk. paper)
   1. Science—Study and teaching. 2. Effective teaching. 3. Motivation in education. I. Title.
Q181.L37 2013
507.1—dc23   2012048351

ISBN 978-0-8077-5421-4 (paper)
ISBN 978-0-8077-5422-1 (hardcover)

Printed on acid-free paper
Manufactured in the United States of America

20   19   18   17   16   15   14   13   8   7   6   5   4   3   2   1

For Melissa, Casey, and Amani

Contents

Foreword

I recall the first time I met Douglas Larkin. He arrived in Madison, Wisconsin after a stint in the Peace Corps in Kenya and a teaching job in Trenton, New Jersey. He and his wife were pursuing master's degrees in science education. Doug, a certified physics teacher was working as a teaching assistant in the University of Wisconsin–Madison's chemistry department. However, the question on his mind was why is it that some students do not persist in science beyond the basic life sciences or biology courses. In other words, "Why aren't more African American and Latino students taking chemistry and physics?" Although Doug had an opportunity to study with world-class science educators he really wanted to work with me. When I explained to him that I could not provide him much intellectual support for his work in science education he told me, "I probably know all the science I need to know. I need to know how to support diverse groups of students in these higher-level science courses. There is nothing so profound about physics that should keep them out of it."

I initially agreed to work with Doug alongside his adviser. I really did not feel comfortable taking over the adviser role. In a little over a year he successful defended his master's thesis and was preparing to return to classroom teaching. Although I spoke with him about pursuing a PhD, Doug was relatively certain that he wanted more classroom experience. With a master's degree in science education, an undergraduate degree in the sciences, and a teaching credential in secondary physics and chemistry, Doug was a "hot commodity" for most public school systems. Fully certified physics teachers are hard to come by. Those with an interest and preparation in physics have many career choices beyond teaching—research and industrial. Doug had his pick of teaching jobs. High schools in his native Trenton were calling with wonderful job offers, mostly in neighborhoods serving high income, high-achieving students. However, Doug chose an offer from one of the poorest, low-achieving schools in the public school district.

Over the next few years Doug stayed in touch with me and uploaded videos of his students learning physics. One video I remember involved his students measuring the rate at which cars were traveling down the street in front of the school. The point of the exercise was to determine whether or not the school community should advocate for a stop light in front of the school Rather than engage the students in a physics "exercise," Doug was helping them understand how their scientific knowledge could be put to use for social/civic purposes. In my work I call this "culturally relevant pedagogy." Doug had found a real problem on which the students could work and helped them understand how their scientific knowledge could help them solve the problem. None of the integrity of the science was compromised. Theirs was a real life physics problem and they needed to figure out how to solve it. Doug was a wonderful example of the "transformation" I believe teachers in diverse settings must experience in order to be empathetic and intellectually rigorous with students regardless of their circumstances. As a Peace Corps volunteer Doug had placed himself in an environment where he had to be resourceful and imaginative to get his job done. He could not complain about parents who were not supportive, students who were disrespectful, or administrators who were unreasonable. He learned that his work required him to use his mind to create curriculum and learning experiences for students and that he was engaged in what William Ayers calls, "intellectual and ethical work." Teaching is not about "being nice" to students or making them "feel good" or even "keeping them in order." In this volume, Doug sets out to describe the "transformation" (or even lack of it) that occurs with prospective teachers through traditional teacher education programs.

When Doug decided to return to graduate school to pursue his doctoral degree he wanted to know about the process of teacher knowledge that was deployed for pedagogical change. He decided that he would not pursue a doctoral degree in science education but rather one in multicultural education. Again he felt that he knew quite a bit about the teaching of science. What he did not know was why so many African American and Latino students were opting out of higher-level science courses. He decided that the answer lay in how teachers were thinking about and teaching science.

Like Christopher Emdin's (Teachers College) notion of science-mindedness, Doug was convinced that the students had the intellectual capacity to master chemistry and physics. He just was not certain that their teachers thought they did. His work on teacher thinking gives an "inside-out" perspective on how teachers' approach teaching science, particularly those teachers who recognize the need to better serve those students who traditionally have not been successful in science (and mathematics). Like Greg Michie (Concordia University, Chicago), Doug carefully documents new (and prospective) teachers' struggle with social justice issues. However, as a science educator his work is complicated by the traditions of science education that maintain a perspective that science learning in areas such as chemistry and physics is only for "some" students.

Larkin's text is an important contribution to a field that has long avoided issues of diversity, difference, and multiculturalism. Instead, it has relied on "scientific knowledge" as the only arbiter of epistemology and validity. In *Deep*

Knowledge, Larkin breaks out of a binary to explore the many possibilities that real learning can give both teachers and students.

—Gloria Ladson-Billings
University of Wisconsin–Madison

Acknowledgments

I wish to publicly express my gratitude to all of the people who made this work possible, and must begin by thanking Jonathan Kozol, whose own work made it impossible for me *not* to be a teacher. Undoubtedly he has carried on many correspondences over the years with teachers who have written to him, but I particularly value the one he carried on with me as a new teacher, first in New Jersey and later as a Peace Corps volunteer in Kenya.

Though I will resist naming them explicitly because I have promised them anonymity, I wish to thank the student teachers, cooperating teachers, university supervisors, principals, and teacher educators who have opened their classrooms, schools, and lives to me throughout the course of this study. In particular I wish to thank Tyler, Armando, Jethro, Kathy, Corrine, Roberta—as well as the other preservice science teachers I followed whose stories are not told here—for permitting me to document their journeys into teaching.

I am grateful for the support of John and Tashia Morgridge, whose generous dissertation fellowship supported me in the final year of my research. I am also thankful that I was able to bounce around ideas and early chapters with my fellow graduate students at UW–Madison, including: Sarah Adumat, Vonzell Agosto, Andrea Anderson, Kevin Anderson, Kathryn Bender, Bethany Brent, Kahaema Byer, Phillip Caldwell II, Hilary Conklin, Julie Cunningham, Kevin Cunningham, Alexa Dimick, Stephanie Eastwood, Ryan Flessner, Wangari Gichiru, Sara Hagen, Beth Hutchinson, Bryn Jaastad, Rachel Lancor, Terri Larson, Steve Laubach, Katrina Liu, Becca Lowenhaupt, David Meshoulam, Connie North, Laura Paige, Lirio Patton, Manali Sheth, Nancy Ruggeri, Carl Whiting, Anjela Wong, and Brian Zoellner.

There were others who offered me guidance and assistance, and I wish to express my appreciation to them here: Kate Abitz, Andy Anderson, Craig Berg, Bryan Barzaga, Bryan Brown, Herb Brunkhorst, Earl Dunovant, Liesl Hohenshell, Kathleen Greene, Mariana Hewson, Mary Kennedy, Katelyn Krueger, Nancy Irvin, Larry Irvin, Dan Marsh, Misty Sato, Amy Schiebel, Ray Scolavino, Christine Sleeter, Russ Smith, Steve Spatucci, Carl Stolz, Barbara Todd, Joe Wells, and Mark Windschitl.

This work would not have been possible without advice and support from the fantastic faculty and staff at the University of Wisconsin–Madison, who made time for my questions and from whom I learned so much: Kathy Blomker, Noah Feinstein, Beth Graue, Mary-Louise Gomez, Erica Halverson, Steve Head, Diana Hess, Alan Lockwood, Cathy Middlecamp, Gary Price, Simone Schweber, Jim Stewart, Bob Tabachnick, and Anita Wager. I am especially grateful to Rich Halverson for his philosophical and practical encouragement, Ken Zeichner for his guidance and model of scholarship, Peter Hewson for the gentle wisdom and opportunities to learn he continues to provide me, Carl Grant for his patient and wholehearted teaching, and John Rudolph for always having an open door, an open ear, and valuable advice. I reserve special thanks to my advisor Gloria Ladson-Billings, who has always been there when I needed her, and time and again has handed me new frames for looking at the world as a scholar, as an activist, and as a parent.

I am indebted to a number of other people who helped make this book possible. In particular, I would like to thank Bill Ayers for his valuable guidance and encouragement; Emily Renwick, Meg Hartmann, Jennifer Baker, Beverly Rivero, Carole Saltz, and the other good people at Teachers College Press for ably shepherding me through the publication process. I also greatly appreciate the support of my new colleagues at Montclair State University during the process of writing this book.

I am deeply grateful to the many people who read the early versions of this manuscript and whose feedback strengthened the final product considerably, including Gail Perry-Ryder, Juan Torres, Susan Eckert, Chris Higgins, and my sister Julia Larkin. Special thanks to my cousin Susannah Reid and my mom, Barbara Ryan Larkin, whose detailed readings and red pens made this work immeasurably better. Any errors that remain are my own, but this book would certainly not have been possible without the support of such wonderful people.

I reserve the greatest thanks for my family, including my in-laws, Richard and Bette Naud, and Jane Dittmer, my fantastic grandmother-in-law. I also thank my own parents, Barbara and John Larkin, whose love and support provided the "roots and wings" for this work. For Casey and Amani, I am simply thankful every day that I get to be your dad. Any night in the past three years when you walked out to the kitchen after bedtime and saw me at the table working on my laptop, it was this book I was writing.

Last, but certainly not least, I wish to express my deepest and most sincere thanks to Melissa Naud, my partner for life. Your support, patience, and good humor throughout this whole endeavor is beyond measure, and words cannot express how much I appreciate all of the things you do that make our shared journey as wonderful as it is.

Introduction

> To the scientist, the universality of physical laws makes the cosmos a marvelously simple place. By comparison, human nature—the psychologist's domain—is infinitely more daunting.
>
> —Neil DeGrasse Tyson (2007)

For some reason, I had never learned how to use a Van de Graaff generator, even though it seemed like something quite basic that every physics teacher should know. I left college feeling that way about a lot of things, actually. I knew that I was going to have to teach static electricity sooner or later, and to do so without the use of my school's Van de Graaff generator—the *pièce de résistance* of science teacher toys—simply because I didn't know how to use it would have been a serious shirking of duty.

I had originally been hired to teach chemistry, though my physical science certification allowed me to teach physics and other courses as well. With my one and only year of college chemistry in the distant past, I had done a great deal of scrambling to catch up and often did twice as much homework as my students did. I relearned moles, gas laws, and stoichiometry, and occasionally pondered why my mastery of upper-level topics in quantum mechanics was of so little value in my day-to-day teaching. That first year, I leaned heavily on other teachers' handouts and labs.

The following year, when I was asked to teach physics, I experienced the same thing. I thought my teaching life would be much easier as a result of graduating as a physics major, but it wasn't. Things I thought I knew, I didn't. Things I definitely knew, I didn't know how to teach. When I mentioned this to other teachers, I would get a knowing smile, regardless of what subject they taught, and an affirmation that they had all started out the same way. Many teachers told me, "You learn as you go," but having witnessed my share of less-than-inspired science teaching, I wondered if that was really true.

As the spring approached, so did the electricity and magnetism unit. I had every intention of asking the other physics teacher at the school to give me a lesson on how to work the Van de Graaff, but somehow never got around to it. Perhaps it had something to do with the fact that he had been my own physics teacher and I was teaching in my former high school. Undoubtedly, part of me wanted the pleasure of figuring it out for myself, yet another part felt too embarrassed to ask for help at all. Wasn't this something I was supposed to know already?

One day after school I was poking around the physics lab in search of some stopwatches when I came across a Van de Graaff generator in a wooden cabinet. The aluminum dome was stored as two hemispheres, and as I pulled the pieces out to look at them I decided that if I was ever going to use the machine in front of students, I ought to make an honest attempt at learning how to work it.

A Van de Graaff generator used properly is a marvelous device. First developed in 1929 by Robert Van de Graaff at Princeton University as a source for the high-voltage particles used to study atoms, it has since become a staple of physics classes and science museums the world over. When set in motion, a rubber belt on a motor transfers charges at a high voltage to an insulated dome. When a second dome is placed nearby and connected to a grounding wire, the charged dome sends an impressive blue spark of miniature lightning across the air gap. This machine never fails to nourish my sense of wonder.

One common demonstration of the Van de Graaff generator involves inviting a volunteer to place a hand on the dome while the machine is turned off. The generator is then switched on, and the person's hair slowly rises until it stands straight on end in all directions. Some adventurous demonstrators go further and create class-wide pulses of current through a human chain of volunteers. These and other impressive demonstrations provide a great variety of static electricity phenomena to be explored, especially in the hands of a skilled teacher. In short, a Van de Graaff generator is a source of both static charge and good fun.

If it works, that is. As I set up the generator, I felt a faint and familiar apprehension about working with electricity. Of course I knew all about electricity from my college coursework. The names of the important laws rolled off my tongue: Ohm's, Coulomb's, Kirchoff's. I could draw circuit diagrams, demonstrate the right-hand rule, and solve inverse square electric force problems with ease. This made me feel even more fraudulent when confronted by a real piece of electrical demonstration equipment. I was all theory and I knew it.

I don't blame anyone for the fact that I graduated as a physics major with almost no practical experience in electricity. Some of the labs I had done as a student teacher with my cooperating teacher's advanced physics class were brand new to me, and it seemed reasonable that there was so much to learn; even five and a half years as an undergraduate couldn't be enough. I figured that I'd just have to learn the things I didn't know as I went along.

I took off my watch—suspecting a ghastly digital chronocide if I didn't—and looked for a switch on the Van de Graaff generator. There wasn't one, so I just pushed in the plug. The contraption rumbled to life. I nudged the second dome to within six inches, and a spark shot across. Then another. And another. The sound was like a second hand on a rumbling metallic clock. There was a whiff of ozone in the air, and the whitish-blue sparks were a spectacle to behold.

As a new science teacher, I lived for these moments. I sincerely felt accomplished whenever I dripped nitric acid onto a copper penny to make poisonous brown nitrogen dioxide or ignited lycopodium powder blown through a funnel to make a huge classroom fireball. At the time, these practices fulfilled my expectations that my identity as a science teacher depended heavily on playing with dangerous artifacts in the pursuit of knowledge. And like many new teachers, I gave substantially less thought to how exactly I expected my students to learn science content from these wonderful demonstrations.

The sparks continued and the air around me crackled with static; just being nearby made the hair on my arms stand up. I watched it run for a while and decided to try making my hair stand on end by placing my hand on the dome. Knowing I would need a fresh start, I unplugged the generator and let it "cool down." In retrospect, this was not a good way to think about static charge. I waited a few moments, then put my hand tentatively on the dome and ZAP! While not completely unanticipated, I had hoped to keep the unpleasant shocks to a minimum. That was overly optimistic.

My first few attempts to get my hair to stand up met with failure and repeated shocks, until I remembered that a stool was involved somehow. I quickly found one in the prep room—it was a Plexiglas board with four insulating feet. I placed it on the floor in front of the generator and stepped up. To my delight, as soon as I started the generator my hair stood on end. That is, an excess of charge built up on each one of my hairs and they all repelled each other until they were standing up; the force of the electric field on each hair was much stronger than the force due to gravity.

It was then I realized that I was stuck. Without the stool, the charge must have been leaking through my shoes to the floor and therefore little had built up on my body during the earlier attempts. But now that I was insulated from the ground, it was clear that the surface of my body had risen to a regrettably high electric potential, which continued to increase with each passing second. The Van de Graaff kept chugging away, and I had no way to stop it other than by pulling the plug (thereby getting a shock) or by pulling my hand away (thereby getting a shock).

I decided to at least stop increasing the amount of charge on myself. I quickly pulled away my hand and received a shock that was both painful and fascinating. I stood on the Plexiglas stool wondering what to do next. The air crackled menacingly while the generator continued to chug along. I figured that no matter what I did, I was going to get shocked again. I reached for the cord with dread, wondering if the term "shock" still applies if you know it's coming. I gripped the insulated plug and yanked hard, grimly accepting the charge that knocked me backward into the chalkboard.

I decided to pack it in, having been electrocuted enough for one afternoon. I pondered my situation as I disassembled the mirror I had clamped to a ring stand, irritated by the feeling of defeat. I wanted my students to know that electricity was understandable, despite the fact that I didn't really seem to understand it at all. I wanted them to learn how to differentiate between electricity that was manageable and electricity that should be feared, but clearly I wasn't even sure of the difference myself. Though the shocks had seemed randomly mischievous to me, I didn't want my students to think of electricity this way. I certainly did not intend to teach them the fine art of being stoic after a dozen shocks. I stopped cleaning up and tried to think rationally about everything that had just happened.

Pausing momentarily, I stepped onto the stool and tried to visualize the electrons. I followed them in my mind as they jumped off the brush and were carried upwards on the rubber belt. I put my hand on the now quiet dome to think about the distribution of charge across its surface. *ZAP!* I had forgotten that the machine had been running for a bit before being unplugged. It felt like the first completely unfair shock of the afternoon, and I swore like a sailor. There simply had to be a better way of discharging the dome.

It was then that I remembered what I was missing. I had seen a curved metal rod, two of them actually, in a drawer somewhere and recalled that their function was somehow related to the Van de Graaff generator. They weren't hard to find, and I quietly thanked the other physics teacher for his neatly organized prep room. Note to veteran teachers: This is how you *really* help your newly certified colleagues who are too proud to ask you how to do things—organize, label, and be trusting with keys.

I got zapped a few more times before I got the hang of the proper sequence: the first step was to ground myself with the rods on the metal sink faucet before stepping off the platform, then ground the dome again before putting a hand on it. I even found a fluorescent tube and some cheerleader pom-poms, which I incorporated into my demonstration plan. I was back to having fun.

As I put everything away, confident that I wouldn't embarrass myself too much in front of my class, I thought about how learning to use the Van de Graaff wasn't really that much different from some other self-teaching I've had to do as a science teacher. It was only the degree of pain that differed. Electric shocks were much less excruciating than standing in front of a class and writing the wrong formula on the board.

Eight years later, I took a job teaching high school physics in Trenton, New Jersey, and was pleasantly surprised to be assigned to the very same classroom where I had done my "junior" student teaching practicum a decade earlier. My classes were much more racially and ethnically diverse than they had been at my former high school, and most of the students at my new school qualified for free or reduced lunch—an indication that many of the students' families lived in poverty. Yet the mood of the school was upbeat, partially buoyed by an atmosphere of noticeable reforms driven by a series of state Supreme Court decisions that had led to an unprecedented amount of state aid to the district.

My classes kept me wonderfully busy, but one of my favorite between-period hobbies was what I liked to think of as "prep room archaeology." Years of benign neglect and use as a general storeroom had left my back room full of unexplored physics treasures, often found in locked drawers or cabinets that took much patience and the occasional hand tool to open. I was regularly rewarded with lab kits from the 1960s, probeware I could attach to my salvaged Macintosh computers, and electronic components whose original use I could only guess. In the very back was a Van de Graaff generator, peeking out from behind boxes on a top shelf. I was happy to see my old round-headed aluminum friend, and resolved to clean my way to that corner before the static electricity unit in the spring.

By the time I reached the machine months later, I had also unearthed the grounding rods, an insulating stool, and another dome. One day after school, I plugged in the Van de Graaff, and it ran for about 2 minutes before the worn and brittle rubber belt broke. Before I put the equipment away—on a newly labeled and uncluttered shelf—I looked up the part number in the science catalog and wrote it on the order list I kept taped on the wall near my desk. The value of thinking long term had been impressed upon me by the veteran teachers I admired.

The following spring, I asked for volunteers in my physics class to step onto the stool and put their hands on the Van de Graaff dome. It was then that I was struck with a thought that had never occurred to me: Every Van de Graaff demonstration I had ever seen had been done with White kids. Every picture I had ever seen in textbooks, every science museum billboard, and every student I had ever called up in my own classes to put a hand on the dome had been White. Though not all had long straight hair, those who did had always put on the best show for their classmates.

I was only four miles away from the nearly all-White suburban high school I had attended and where I first worked as a teacher, yet owing to the intense racial segregation that exists between school districts in New Jersey, none of the students in my Trenton class that day—let alone the ones raising their hands to volunteer—were White. A brief moment of panic set in, and I wondered if the demonstration would even work. Might my beloved physics demonstration have a built-in racial bias? Would my African American, Asian, Latino, and Latina students get to have the same science fun as the White kids down the road?

Of course, it was far too late to back out of the demonstration, and so I simply picked an eager student and carried on. I need not have worried, for just as with White students, some kids' hair stood up better than others. In time I relearned what I already knew: The demonstration worked best on days when the air was dry, and hair would stand up provided it was free to move around and long enough to do so.

My thinking about using demonstrations for teaching had also changed by this time, mostly as a result of what I had learned as a graduate student in science education courses. In my first years of teaching I would have been content with just putting on a performance and hoping my students would learn the physics. I now had my students actively engaged in thinking about the science phenomena, working in groups to construct a conceptual model of what was happening at the level of electrons. I was now much more intentional as a teacher in what I wished my students to learn from my "magic shows."

Long afterward, I continued to reflect on that one moment of uncertainty when I did not know if the demonstration would work with my non-White students' hair. What if I had been fearful about the potential consequences of a failed demonstration and simply skipped it? What if I hadn't known how to operate the equipment the first time I used it and had erroneously ascribed any failure to perform properly to the demographic characteristics of my students? What other decisions had I made about teaching that were based on unconsidered assumptions?

Science is so often presented to students as a fixed body of facts, yet in that moment, my ability to teach science depended on so much more than my knowledge of static electricity. What I knew (and did not know) about my subject, about my students, and about how people learn science had all influenced my actions in the classroom that day. Another example of this kind of classroom decision making occurred in my classroom two years later, and it also involved Dr. Van de Graaff's wondrous invention.

I was all set to begin the Van de Graaff generator demonstration with my physics students when a fight outside the door interrupted class. My students remained in their seats while I stepped out into the hallway to clear away bystanders. The security guards had responded quickly and wrenched the two girls apart, but not before they had ripped the weave out of each other's hair.

Growing up, I had known nothing about hair weave and still understood little beyond the fact that adding hair extensions was an expensive and time-consuming ritual. The first time I had ever encountered weave was in my twenties when a friend and I visited a rehearsal studio and I noticed that one of the musicians—a White guy—had the longest and straightest hair I had ever seen. My friend had a good laugh later explaining to me what hair extensions were and why people in certain heavy metal bands loved them.

For many of my students, I was certain that hair weave had a cultural significance beyond simple appearances. I had also come to understand that—at least for a White male teacher like me—the number one rule of hair weave is that one does not talk about hair weave. My African American chemistry students had taught me this much when I had first started talking with them about it during a unit on polymers. I was informed that asking a student about hair weave was considered an impolite topic of conversation for a teacher to ask his students, akin perhaps to the inappropriateness of the question, "Boxers or briefs?"

With the hallway returning to normal after the fight, Mr. Wilson, a White English teacher, picked up the pile of fake hair as I shooed the remaining students back to class. "What do I do with this?" he asked me. Mr. Wilson held the hair in his hands as if it were a fragile gift. We both just stared at it. "Do you think either of them will want this back?" he asked. I didn't know, but one of the combatants was a freshman in my first period class so I agreed to hold on to it long enough to ask her. He piled the hair into my cupped hands and I opened the door with my elbow.

The class whooped with laughter at the sight of me. I paused, wondering where to put the hair, and the class quieted down. I was heading toward the front desk when I remembered what I had been about to do before the fight broke out. My students must have been thinking the same thing because from the back I heard a soft voice call "Do it." (Eric, if you're reading this, I'm pretty sure it was you.) I stood there with the handful of hair, looking at the aluminum dome of the Van de Graaff. The chorus slowly grew, as did the laughter. I kept looking between the weave in my hands and the generator and finally relented.

I placed the pile of hair on top of the dome and switched the generator on. With the sphere itself like a head, the hair slowly rose up, and the lightest pieces launched outward into the air as if a hair dryer was blowing every direction at once. The class erupted like never before, and many of my students whipped out their cell phones—totally forbidden in school of course, but I was good at pretending not to see them—and snapped pictures. When I turned off the generator and the hair remained on end, the class began to ask why, first to me and then to each other. After 10 minutes of exquisite classroom debate—the upright hair motionless on the dome all the while—they had figured it out to their satisfaction as well as mine. I handed the grounding rods to a student, who walked toward the front desk with the measured movements of someone determined to avoid a shock. The other students fell silent with suspense as she gently touched the linked rods as I had showed her, first to the dome and then to the cold water pipe. When the electrostatically suspended hair collapsed without a sound, the class broke into wild applause.

The way I thought about science, about students, and even about what constituted teaching had changed considerably over the decade since my first uncertain months as a teacher. Not only would I have likely missed taking advantage of a culturally relevant teachable moment as a new teacher, I wouldn't even have been comfortable enough with the subject matter to realize that I could place the burden of figuring things out on the students. How had this change happened?

I was hardly convinced it could simply be called "learning as you go." How did all the different bits of what I knew interact with one another to help me make teaching decisions? Would it have been possible for my teacher education program to prepare me to be such an adventurous teacher in my first years? I decided that it would be worthwhile to try to figure out how people *actually* learned to teach high school science, because from what I had seen and experienced, there was a genuine need to better prepare science teachers for the diverse classrooms in which they would work. This book is the result of my search for answers.

CHAPTER 1

The Puzzle of Learning to Teach

In this book I present the stories of six people in university programs learning to teach science in middle and high school classrooms. My hope is that these accounts will be most valuable for those whose own stories of learning to teach are still unfolding, no matter how far in the past those first days as a teacher may be. These cases show how teachers' personal webs of interconnected ideas change over time, and in crafting them I have chosen to pay the greatest attention to what they tell us about the enduring challenges of preparing science teachers to teach for both understanding and equity.

The inherent difficulty of learning to teach science for understanding is well known, even by master science teachers. It is one thing for a teacher to be a transmitter of information, but it is another matter entirely to ensure that students understand scientific topics flexibly and deeply. It is no secret that part of what makes this so difficult for student teachers is the fact that they are often still learning the content themselves. Even with high grades in college science coursework, a prospective teacher is likely to have only a narrow route of understanding through his or her content. Straying from that path increases the hazard of becoming lost in thickets of uncertain knowledge, a harrowing prospect for many novices.

Then there is the challenge of learning to teach in a way that leads to equitable outcomes for students. Though the lives and experiences of teachers may differ from many of their students' with respect to gender, race, social class, ethnicity, sexual orientation, language, abilities, and culture, they are still expected to be effective in teaching everyone. These differences have pedagogical implications, and figuring out when and how student diversity matters is undoubtedly challenging for new teachers.

Coming to terms with this pair of issues is at the heart of the intellectual work of teaching. Resolving them is what makes a good teacher different from any other knowledgeable and caring adult. With a richer understanding of how teacher thinking develops, secondary science teachers can be prepared to teach for both understanding and equity in a more intentional, effective, and enduring manner.

BECOMING A TEACHER

It is often difficult, even painful, to watch student teachers in the classroom. They make novice mistakes such as saying "like" 50 times in a single lesson. They talk too much. They miss important cues from students. They are unaware of counterintuitive strategies that would work brilliantly. They practice teaching as the controlled delivery of information. They sometimes get their content wrong. Even the most talented among them lapse into familiar childhood patterns of "playing school" in moments of crisis or doubt. Some are unnecessarily harsh; others acquiesce to their students' slightest whims. And all too often, the students simply aren't asked to do anything while the student teacher "teaches."

Yet the discomfort I feel whenever I observe student teachers—which is often these days—has little to do with any of these issues, important as they are. It has more to do with the fact that learning to teach is an intensely personal process that, by its very nature, must be done in public. When I watch student teachers learning to teach, I am also witnessing them confront challenges to their identity, beliefs, and values, often at the limits of their knowledge. Some recognize that they are being challenged this way; others do not. Regardless, their private struggles are in full view, a situation that does not commonly occur in modern times outside of parenthood and reality television. I feel an embarrassment rooted in empathy: I was making those mistakes not so long ago.

Part of the nature of learning to teach is that people come with their own ideas about teaching, learning, and the purposes of education. They also bring their personal beliefs, professional goals, and conceptions about the nature and organization of their disciplinary subject matter. Perhaps most important, they carry with them the history of their own life experiences. All of these things form the raw material from which one learns to teach. The rough and tumble of classroom life alone is insufficient for fashioning this material into a competent teacher, as even those who champion the trial-by-fire method of learning to teach on the job are well aware. This raw material—this clay of one's conceptions—changes only when it is worked by intentions, shaped by conscious examination, and tested by action.

Learning to teach is still sometimes portrayed as a skill-based apprenticeship, and student teaching itself is rooted in this tradition. Implicit in this view is that learning to teach occurs as a result of simply accumulating experience under the guidance of an expert who provides critical feedback. Consequently, tips and tricks of master teachers are coins of the realm, valued by novices over most everything else because they are a currency that can be spent. Certain skills are undoubtedly crucial for learning to teach, but framing teacher education as mostly a process of skill acquisition may misrepresent much of the real work of becoming a teacher.

Learning to teach involves an investment of serious intellectual effort into the nature of one's own knowledge and beliefs. Prospective teachers usually hold some idea of what good teaching looks like and then seek to cultivate the skills needed to put that vision into practice. Questioning that vision of good teaching does not come easily, and neither does challenging the underlying assumptions about knowledge, learning, and society upon which it depends.

Over the last three decades, great effort has gone into identifying the knowledge, skills, and beliefs that teachers need in order to teach all of their students. As important as this task has been, less attention has been paid to figuring out the ways that prospective teachers actually learn these things. The rise of the standards movement in the United States first in the PreK–12 curriculum and then in teacher education, is emblematic of this contradiction. In the best circumstances, setting standards represents a crucial step in a democratic process of negotiating shared goals for education. Yet the act of making these lists of knowledge, skills, beliefs, attitudes, and dispositions says frustratingly little about how someone might acquire them.

As a result of research across many different disciplines, we know a great deal more about student learning than we did 50 years ago, and much of this can be usefully applied to teacher education (Hammerness et al., 2005). We understand that new knowledge does not simply accumulate during learning but rather interacts with the existing ideas of the learner (Bransford, Brown, & Cocking, 1999). We know the importance of language and culture in structuring cognition (Heath, 1983; Lakoff & Johnson, 1980), and we understand that issues of power are never far from the enactment of curriculum and instruction (Anyon, 2005; Apple, 2000).

Teacher educators have designed many strategies to shift the thinking of prospective teachers in desired directions: Readings, lectures, discussions, structured tasks, classroom visits, field experiences, data collection, written reflections, and portfolio work all serve to guide prospective teachers toward a particular vision of good teaching. The problem is that the "knowledge base" for teaching, now richly developed and carefully organized (Darling-Hammond, Baratz-Snowden, & National Academy of Education, 2005), does not always fit with the way teachers think about their own teaching, as the cases in this book will illustrate.

In their teaching practice, as well as in their lives, teachers have a hierarchy of issues that are important to them, including archetypal needs such as freedom, belonging, power, fun, and even survival. These may guide what they do in the classroom as much as, or perhaps even more than, the priorities of their teacher education programs do. New teachers may also realize quite suddenly that there are a whole host of other nitty-gritty details about the school itself—such as who holds the keys to the microscope cabinets—that have the potential to affect the quality of their classroom teaching.

LEARNING TO TEACH AS A PROCESS
OF CONCEPTUAL CHANGE

The notion that individuals acquire or build knowledge for teaching, as if they are collecting toy blocks to assemble a tall tower, bears little if any resemblance to the real and messy processes by which people really learn to teach. It is usually a long, difficult, and meandering journey, because learning to teach involves the reorganization of a lifetime's worth of knowledge.

An idea held since childhood, such as *plants take in carbon dioxide and give off oxygen*, can suddenly become an organizing conception with explanatory power to a new biology teacher, with monumental implications for her teaching (as will be shown in Corrine's case.) Conversely, previous conceptions that seemed unalterable, such as *my students must listen to me if they are to learn*, can seem much less plausible when a teacher attends closely to how her students actually learn (as will be shown in Kathy's case).

As human beings, we naturally treat new ideas with skepticism because our existing conceptions generally do a good job in helping us explain and understand our world. This is why the term "misconception" can be misleading. What one person considers a misconception can be a perfectly reasonable and satisfying idea to someone else, and vice-versa. To accept a new idea as true, it is usually necessary for a person to become less satisfied with the original idea as currently held (Hewson & Lemberger, 2000; Posner, Strike, Hewson, & Gertzog, 1982).

For example, the common belief that a heavy object falls much faster than a light one can be called into question by dropping a tennis ball and a soccer ball from an identical height simultaneously and watching them hit the ground together. However, any new idea ought to be understandable, make sense, and feel right to be considered a candidate to replace the old one. In the ball example, the new idea might be: *The weight of an object has little effect on how fast it falls.* Of course, the new idea might not be expressed in exactly the way a textbook or scientist would express it; it might even be quite wrong! But if the new idea is intelligible, plausible, and has greater explanatory power than does the old, it will likely take hold as an organizing conception. All the better if a new idea explains more than the older one, such as when Newton saw that his equations for free fall also explained the moon's orbit around the Earth.

It is helpful to think about each idea we hold in our minds as fitting into its own niche, much like those of individual organisms in an ecological system. The philosopher Stephen Toulmin and others envisioned this interrelatedness of conceptions within a single person's mind as a *conceptual ecology* (Hewson, 1985; Toulmin, 1972). Our ideas connect to and depend on one another, and like a real ecosystem, this conceptual ecology is stable and robust while also being active and ever-changing. Learning to teach, viewed in this manner, cannot be a linear process because a change on one side of the ecological web reverberates throughout the whole system, albeit sometimes rather slowly.

Teachers access this conceptual ecology of ideas almost continuously in their practice as problems arise and decisions need to be made. The ways in which teachers define problems of practice are influenced greatly by their existing web of ideas, which then give shape to the solutions they seek. For example, a teacher frustrated by her students' inability to turn in homework may see the problem as one of student motivation and decide that a more strict homework policy is needed. A different framing of the problem might lead her to rethink the nature of tasks students are asked to complete at home. As the cases in this book will show, the ability to reframe problems of practice is an essential element for teachers' professional growth.

LEARNING TO TEACH CHANGES YOU. WILL YOU LET IT?

As a preservice teacher nearly 20 years ago, I had not accorded any weight at all to the concept of "learning to teach" other than as a bureaucratic hoop to be jumped through. As a new teacher, my focus was on preparing for each class and doing the things I thought that high school science teachers were supposed to do. This included setting up equipment for labs, practicing chemical demonstrations ahead of time, and writing out every step of difficult homework problems (with units!) so that my students could check their answers. I also coached cross-country and track, tutored math twice a week at an urban community center, developed after-school math and science clubs for my own students, and organized poetry slams and rock concerts in the community—all things I considered important to my identity as a good teacher. I saw these activities as part of a larger agenda to contribute to the well-being of my students and society. I also happened to be single and without children of my own at the time, making a great deal of that activity possible. In those first years as a teacher, I found that the victories were mostly small ones that didn't seem to compensate for the monumental investment of time and energy it took to teach.

I would later feel the same way during my first few months in Kenya. It felt good having learned enough Swahili to buy a soda, but that wasn't why I had joined the Peace Corps. I had been a new science teacher in New Jersey for only 2 years before leaving for East Africa, and had found adjusting to the culture of the school to be the most difficult part of my experience. Living without electricity and learning a new language had been surprisingly straightforward. My school, on the other hand, was as complex a system as I'd ever encountered. I took to heart the sign above our Peace Corps trainer's desk that read, "People usually act rationally, but it's up to YOU to find the rationale."

Having found my footing after the first year, I was honored to be invited to work for a few days with a new cohort of science, math, and English teachers at the Peace Corps training center. Though all were certified teachers in the United States, none had experience in Kenyan classrooms, and part of my role was to offer a view of what they might expect when they were placed in schools there. I had not planned to cause any trouble.

After some small group sessions with the science teachers in the morning, one of the trainers asked me if I would like to give feedback on the trainees' practice lessons that afternoon. I agreed, and later that day a number of the teachers took turns teaching mini-lessons on content from the Kenyan national curriculum. After each lesson, the trainer and I shared our thoughts and observations, talking through some of the issues that we thought might arise in Kenyan classrooms.

One math teacher taught a very entertaining, hands-on lesson about the volumes and surface areas of geometric shapes. He was energetic, confident, and well prepared—the kind of math teacher my high school principal friends hire in a heartbeat. In the discussion afterward I noted that such a lesson would probably go over very well in a U.S. classroom, but in Kenyan schools, students would likely feel that they had not been taught anything because there had been little to write down and memorize. It was a counter intuitive and hard-won lesson I had learned over the past year.

Later that evening, the trainer handed me a very angry letter from the math teacher. He was livid about my criticism and accused me of unfairly berating him in front of his peers simply for being a progressive educator who wanted his students to have a constructivist experience with mathematics. Apparently, my critique had pushed him past his breaking point, and the trainer spent a good chunk of that evening talking him out of going back home to California. I came away from the incident humbled, with a deeper appreciation of the profound sense of fragility that many new teachers have about their work, and with no small alarm concerning the unexpected power of my words. I wondered if I would have acted any differently had I been in the math teacher's shoes. For the first time, I considered the possibility that teacher learning was a much more complicated (and therefore attractive) problem than any I had encountered as a physics major.

Over the next decade and a half as I worked in various capacities, first with my peers in high school science departments, then as a student-teacher supervisor in graduate school, and in my present position as a university professor, I have witnessed this same sense of fragility in new teachers again and again, even with the most diplomatically crafted comments from the most sensitive observers. Certainly, feedback on teaching may be resisted if it is not perceived as valid or applicable. Feedback may not even be heard if it fails to speak to individuals in a manner that resonates with the way they see themselves—and in these cases such defensiveness may be justified. But why does this resistance seem to be so common in learning to teach?

One answer suggested by Deborah Britzman (2003) draws upon the notion that the raw materials for crafting teaching practice are teachers' ideas and life experiences. She notes that just as identity influences conceptions about teaching, the reverse is also true. Learning to teach has the potential to affect one's beliefs, knowledge, and goals because of the way it compels the reinterpretation of past experience. This is why learning to teach must be considered more than simply an acquisition of skills; it is also a process of conceptual change.

To put it another way, resisting changes in what you do as a teacher may be rooted in resistance to changing who you are. Intentional conceptual change is also difficult because it depends as much on affective factors such as motivation, interest, and self-efficacy; it need not be a rational process at all (Pintrich, Marx, & Boyle, 1993). In other words, a new idea might make sense, but you just might not feel like changing your mind.

WHAT DO WE MEAN WHEN WE TALK ABOUT DIVERSITY?

Given that one of the central aims of this book is to investigate the ways in which prospective teachers hold and change their ideas about race, ethnicity, and culture, it is necessary to clarify my use of such terms here. As a person who identifies—and is commonly identified—as White, I also do so to establish a reference point for critiques of interpretations that may result from my own biases.

Race

In its statement on race, the American Anthropological Association (AAA Executive Board, 1998) noted that although race currently holds little salience as a biological concept, it retains power as a social construct and distorts ideas about group behavior and human differences, including the idea that cultural behavior is genetically determined.

In this study, questions about race may be viewed as an attempt to probe participants' ideas about the meaning, use, and explanatory power of racial categories and labels. Given that race continues to be a factor in educational inequity, exploring the pedagogical implications of teachers' ideas about race is an important step in understanding how race continues to operate in classrooms.

The pedagogical implications of race examined in this study may be viewed from two different perspectives. The first frames race as an element of human physiology that has genetic markers responsible for the expression of physical and biochemical traits. This view of race may also appear as part of the content in science teaching, as when inherited traits such as skin color are discussed during a genetics unit in a biology class.

The second view positions race as a conceptual scheme with tacit and explicit explanatory power (Conant, 1951). The power of race to serve as a social marker is most visible when it is expected to play an explanatory role, such as in Tatum's (2003) question, "Why are all the Black kids sitting together in the cafeteria?" The rhetorical question, "To this person, what does the concept of race explain?" serves as a powerful analytic tool for probing how people think and act.

Ethnicity

The concept of *ethnicity* is often conflated with race in the teacher education literature (Grant & Agosto, 2006), and therefore requires a bit more definitional precision. Everyday usage of this term and its cognate, *ethnic*, often refer to social groups of common heritage and language. Although ethnicity can take the form of an ascribed label—such as the term "Hispanic" in reference to those whose heredity can be traced to regions where the Spanish language is dominant—these labels may often obscure important cultural, historical, and socioeconomic differences. Longstreet (1997) suggests that ethnicity may be considered as "the part of cultural development that occurs prior to the biological onset of a child's abstract intellectual power" (p. 110), and therefore ethnic identity may be both unconscious and involuntary.

It is relevant to the stories in this book to note that individuals' self-identification by race and ethnicity are often part of governmental data collection efforts, and guidelines published by the U.S. Census Bureau (1997) affirm that the rationale for doing this stems from the responsibility to enforce civil rights laws. Since 2003, these guidelines have stipulated that forms collecting this information must allow individuals to select more than one race or ethnicity if they wish.

Culture

In contrast, the term *culture* is understood and used in a multitude of ways and never appears as a checkbox category on a form. An ethnographic approach to educational research informs the definition of culture used in this study, exemplified by the work of George and Louise Spindler (1990), who write: "We think of 'culture' as a process. It is what happens as people try to make sense of their own lives and sense of the behavior of other people with whom they have to deal," (p. 2). In many respects, this definition of culture can be likened to a scientific paradigm (Kuhn, 1970) in that it orients individuals to interpret phenomena in particular ways.

With respect to teacher education, Ladson-Billings (2006) notes that the concept of culture is apt to be misunderstood by the primarily White and middle-class students who form the largest part of teacher education programs, who have difficulty applying the concept of culture to themselves. She advocates for the use of strategies that enable students to "take a close look at their cultural systems and recognize them for what they are—learned behavior that has been normalized and regularized" (p. 109).

Diversity

Finally, it is important to carefully attend to language in order to ensure that the term *diversity* is not constructed in opposition to an idealized norm (Villegas & Lucas, 2002). In biology, the word *evolution* is often mistakenly applied to individuals, when its proper usage should be in reference only to groups or populations. Similarly, the term "culturally diverse" has been applied to individual students, when the term makes proper sense only when referring to the fact that multiple cultures may be represented within a given group of students or, in the case of classrooms or schools, a shared social space. Nevertheless, far too many authors refer to *culturally diverse students*—a slippery linguistic construction in which the "s" is too easily dropped from this inherently plural term. In this book I use words such as *diversity* and *culturally diverse* in ways that refer to groups that are genuinely and categorically heterogeneous.

In many respects, preparing teachers for diverse classrooms reflects idealism about the ultimate outcomes of efforts to desegregate schools not only in terms of race but also in terms of social class, disability, and other dimensions of diversity. The moral rationale for such desegregation is that these demographic characteristics continue to hold an unconscionable predictive power for academic achievement that would be improbable in a fair system of schooling (Kozol, 2005). Preparing teachers to work for social justice in this way, both in the areas of large-scale reform and in everyday interactions with students, is an important goal for teacher education programs.

LEARNING FROM TEACHERS LEARNING TO TEACH

As a doctoral student in teacher education, I became intrigued with the observation that the misconceptions student teachers held about teaching science often resembled the misconceptions that students developed about scientific concepts. This led me to examine the processes by which these conceptions changed—or did not change—over time as a result of learning to teach.

The participants in this study were all prospective secondary science teachers in one of four different university-based teacher education programs in the United States. They were selected in an effort to maximize the opportunity to learn from the different personal characteristics and life experiences each brought to the task of learning to teach, as well as for their willingness to participate in the research. The demographic characteristics of the participants,[1] including their subject certification areas, are shown in Table 1.1.

Two of the programs were located in large public universities (Briggstown University and Delorenzo University), one in a smaller public institution (Clayton State College), and the last in a small, church-affiliated private college (Acacia College).

Table 1.1. Characteristics of the Student Teachers

Name	Program	Age Range	Gender	Self-Identification (Race/Ethnicity)	Certification(s) Sought
Corrine	Acacia College	35–39	F	White	Biology Broadfield Science
Armando	Briggstown University	20–25	M	Latino/ Dominican Republic	Biology, Chemistry Broadfield Science
Jethro	Briggstown University	50–55	M	White	Physics, Computer Science
Kathy	Briggstown University	25–29	F	White	Biology
Tyler	Clayton State College	20–25	M	White	Biology, Physics
Robbie	Delorenzo University	20–25	F	White	Chemistry

All were located within the same Midwest state and were subject to the same state regulations for teacher preparation. Though these four institutions had programmatic differences among them, all were run by highly qualified science education faculty, and each prepared between 10 and 20 secondary science teachers every year.[2]

The design of this study was influenced by prior research on individuals learning to teach science that also focused on issues of diversity and equity.[3] As valuable as these studies were, I wished to gain a better sense of how and why teacher thinking changes during teacher preparation. In conducting this study, I built upon established teacher education research tools, which included questionnaires and semi-structured interviews.[4] These interviews contained some hypothetical scenarios designed to probe participants' pedagogical reasoning, and were revisited in subsequent interview sessions. In adapting tools for this study, I incorporated some of my own experiences from teaching physics, chemistry, earth science, and biology into the questions and scenarios posed to prospective teachers. For example, I asked prospective physics teachers to imagine that they were conducting a demonstration on electricity involving students' hair and a Van de Graaff generator, and a student asked, "This works better on White people's hair, right?" Responses to this question and similar ones where student diversity had to be invoked in the service of teaching science content often illuminated hidden connections in student teacher thinking across different aspects of teaching.

The stories of the student teachers in this book also give voice to the issues of importance that they themselves brought to the task of learning how to teach. It is my view that learning to teach is an intertwining of two sets of priorities: those of the prospective teacher and those of the teacher educators. I have chosen to tell stories from student teaching because this is the time when conflicts and tensions between these two sets of priorities seem to be greatest.

It was also my intent to highlight connections between domains of each teacher's thinking that might otherwise appear separate—to sketch each person's conceptual ecology, in other words. Rather than evaluate whether prospective teachers changed in the manner intended by their programs, I simply examined what changed in their thinking as a result of learning to teach and tried to situate these changes in the wider conceptual ecology of each individual.[5]

RESEARCH ETHICS AND
THE QUESTION OF INTERVENTION

Throughout this study I strove to minimize my involvement in the teacher education processes I observed, but this was not always possible. When Briggstown students asked me questions about teaching, I tended to inquire about their goals and then direct them toward resources that could be helpful. I always avoided evaluative statements, especially about practice. Yet I also felt an ethical responsibility to make both the process and outcomes of the research worthwhile to those I researched (Smith, 1999), and living up to this commitment took different forms for each participant. For example, Jethro asked me to write him a reference letter that spoke to his competence with instructional technology, Corrine requested feedback on a lesson, and Tyler wanted advice for his job search. I did all of these things without hesitation.

Prior to publishing the cases in this book, I have shared them formally through conferences and journal articles, and informally with colleagues and the prospective teachers with whom I work. I am often asked why I appear to have done little to intervene in some of the more precarious situations that are recounted in these cases. After all, wouldn't my advice have been useful to student teachers as they struggled with the challenges of learning to teach? Couldn't I have helped Jethro with his lesson planning? Couldn't Kathy have used some advice on how to resist a school culture that was hostile to issues of diversity?

There are two answers to this question. The first is perhaps the expected answer, that my detachment from their actions was a necessary aspect of doing research so as to maintain as much objectivity as possible and not compromise my findings. Of course in any study of this sort, the mere presence of a researcher can serve as an intervention, and participants often told me that they had continued to think about the questions I posed to them long after the interviews were over.

My other response is simply that I was patient. It is my belief that one of the greatest challenges for teacher educators is to resist the temptation to revert to transmissionist practices ourselves in the drive to ensure that prospective teachers leave our care with the "right answers" about teaching (Duckworth, 2006). Truly, the real intervention took place after the data was analyzed and the cases were written. Each of the teachers read his or her own case at the end of this process and provided feedback about its authenticity. Together we sought to correct and discuss errors of observation and interpretation, and I made sure that they all felt comfortable with the way I had represented them. In these conversations, we also talked more freely about other interpretations of events, different strategies for teaching particular science topics, and alternate approaches for dealing with some of the issues that arose in their classrooms. It was my impression that the written cases, and our discussions that followed, prompted some of the deepest teacher learning I have ever witnessed. Of course by the time this occurred, I was no longer following them in the classroom, so any claim of teacher learning as a result must be considered anecdotal rather than based on empirical evidence.

INTRODUCTION TO THE CASES

Each case opens with a vignette intended to portray the student teacher's practice for the reader, followed by a summary of his or her experiences in teacher education. I then describe the various changes that took place in each teacher's ideas over the course of the study, particularly at the intersection of ideas about teaching science and conceptions concerning the pedagogical implications of student diversity (Paine, 1990). As will be demonstrated, these ideas often connected in surprising ways to beliefs about learning, the purpose of schooling, scientific practice, and the teachers' own personal lives.

Some classroom settings presented here are more diverse than others, but in each case, the student teachers had the opportunity to work with students who were different from themselves in multiple ways. In some cases, such as those of Corrine or Armando, the individual classes were demographically homogeneous. Yet the presence of even a single student of a different racial, ethnic, or cultural group in a class was enough of a catalyst to prompt participants' thinking about the implications of student diversity on their teaching. Others, such as Kathy and Tyler, had the opportunity to teach introductory as well as advanced science courses, and as a result of the common structural segregation that occurs in such situations (Oakes, 2005), they had the experience of teaching in classes with varying degrees of racial, ethnic, and cultural diversity.

I present publicly reported demographic information about each school within the cases to provide a sense of this context, recognizing that the composition of a single class will often be different from that of the school as a whole, especially given the absence of reliable data on the identities of students in individual classrooms. Any description of students within the cases ought to be considered solely observational and less reliable than the public data.

It took quite a bit of time to give shape to these cases, and I was guided by a sense of empathy as I did so. After all, it was not so long ago that I was the one learning to teach, and my own missteps as a new high school science teacher certainly feel more egregious to me than any presented here.

CHAPTER 2

Tentative Steps Toward Disarming Diversity

Tyler—Biology, Physics

> The issue of race is especially touchy for me. . . . I hate to say it, I'd
> almost be tempted to sacrifice a little bit of good science to protect myself.
> . . . I don't want to lose my job, quite frankly. I like teaching. And this is a
> touchy subject, and it's weird and it's fearful for me.
>
> —Tyler

"Careful," says student teacher Tyler Vaughn, once he stops entering the previous period's attendance momentarily to peer over the computer. "That's real, and someone's leg."

The African American student handling the fibula that had been on the front desk looks at the bone with a mixture of fascination and repulsion before he gently returns it to its place on a stack of papers and lowers himself into his seat without comment. Someone else asks if the leg is "really real" and Tyler nods, affirming that they are studying bones in the anatomy and physiology class. He takes a sip from a coffee mug as the bell rings and raises his voice to the class. "Can everybody have a seat please?"

The room is a hive of social activity, little of which seems related to 10th-grade biology at the moment. Tyler walks back and forth behind the teacher's desk shepherding students to their seats. "Holy cow, we're missing a lot today," he says to the students, who continue to chat amongst themselves. Mr. Gilbert, Tyler's cooperating teacher, is talking with a student in the prep room and is just visible enough for the class to know he is there. He has confidence in Tyler's ability to run the class alone now, and this trust is visible to students and observers alike.

"All right," Tyler says, talking over the students. "You are going to write down nothing today!" He says this with enthusiasm, like a sales pitch. "You're going to be doing an activity today. So the sooner we get rolling . . ."

The chatter continues as Tyler says, "Let me take attendance." It is his fourth month in this classroom and he knows everyone well enough to take attendance silently, but, as I learn from him later, he enjoys the opportunity to make a brief connection with every student by calling each name and making eye contact. The students appear to enjoy the extra time to talk.

After some banter with the students, Tyler removes the lens cap from a computer projector and the title slide of a presentation fills the whiteboard. Tyler uses the first half-dozen slides to discuss the difference between DNA transcription and translation, the topic for the day. Tyler occasionally stops to ask a question to the class as a whole. When the correct answer is eventually said out loud, by either the students or Tyler, the lesson continues.

He shows a short video animation of translation and narrates each step of the DNA translation. Tyler asks, "What does each one of the colors represent?" There are some muffled and half-hearted answers, but not for lack of interest. The video clip is striking in its clear and straightforward representation of the DNA translation process, and the students appear to be fully engaged in watching it, as am I.

"Each color there represents a different amino acid," Tyler states. The words "amino acid" echo in the class softly as some students give a delayed response to his initial question. "When will this process stop?" Tyler asks the room as the ribosome in the video continues to crank out a protein mechanically. The faint words "stop codon" emerge from a corner of the class, and almost simultaneously the image of the protein on the screen breaks free into the cytoplasm. "That's right," says Tyler, "when it reaches the stop codon."

The lights go on and Tyler very matter-of-factly explains the day's task, which is a set of worksheet activities in a packet the students received the previous day. "Your assignment will be to explore the three kinds of mutations: insertions, substitutions, and deletions." These terms, along with their definitions appear on the board with a mouse click. Six students have their notebooks out, while the rest just watch. "I'm actually going to turn you loose on this now," Tyler says. With 15 minutes remaining in class, students form work groups, though not all are actually doing work. Four boys leave the cramped confines of the rows of desks in the front half of the room and spread out at a lab table in the back, and are soon followed by others. A few students work alone in the front, but most appear to be partnered with classmates.

Tyler circulates through the room, checking on students and occasionally refocusing them on the task. One student asks, "Why is this so long and boring?" Tyler replies, "I guarantee this will get more exciting." Another student presses him about whether they could use the microscopes to see this DNA translation "for real." Tyler explains to the student that with the light microscopes in class, it would be difficult to see red blood cells, let alone amino acids.

For the rest of the period, when students call out, "Mr. V!" Tyler is there almost instantly, as if not wanting to miss any opportunity to interact.

Tyler began as an undergraduate in engineering at Delorenzo University, the flagship institution of his state's university system, and then transferred in his junior year to Clayton State. Course requirements for certifications in both biology and physics had put him a semester behind many of his peers in the teacher education program, and as a result he did not complete his full-time student teaching until a full year after he had taken his Methods of Teaching Science course at Clayton State.

His student teaching placement at Central High School in Delorenzo City, the state capital, resulted from a request to work near his home, about an hour's drive from the Clayton State campus. He expressed a cosmopolitan excitement about his assignment, particularly when comparing it to his own high school. He stated in our first interview, "I come from White suburbia, I think we had about two African Americans in a nineteen-hundred person class. Here, it's about fifty-fifty between Caucasians and minorities. This is really neat for me." The demographic data for Central High School for the school year of Tyler's student teaching is shown in Table 2.1.

Tyler's cooperating teacher, Mr. Gilbert, had worked with many student teachers over the years and expressed candidly that this mentoring process was an aspect of his profession that he particularly enjoyed. Though Tyler told me that he would have preferred to ease his way gently into taking over a class, Mr. Gilbert felt strongly that Tyler should start teaching at the beginning of the school year, a decision Tyler said, "was the best thing that could have happened to me." In brief asides during my visits over the semester, Mr. Gilbert always stressed Tyler's competence as a teacher.

Tyler began by taking over two sections of Anatomy and Physiology, an upper-level elective class. There was also a single 10th-grade biology class in the schedule, which he and Mr. Gilbert team-taught for the first two months. In November, Tyler took over the biology class completely and they decided to co-teach the Anatomy and Physiology classes. Tyler and Mr. Gilbert both agreed that becoming

Table 2.1. Enrollment and Race/Ethnicity Data for Tyler's Student Teaching Placement at Central High School

Total Enrollment	American Indian	Asian	Black	Hispanic	White
1,693	0.5%	11.3%	25.9%	10.7%	51.6%

the lead teacher for this group was the most productive use of Tyler's student teaching time, especially given the classroom management challenges the biology students presented.

⬚

Sketching the shifts in Tyler's conceptual ecology entails attending to the ways his thinking both changed and did not change over the course of student teaching. Like all participants in this study, Tyler's priorities and commitments to particular ideas greatly influenced how he interpreted events in his classroom, and his willingness and ability to examine some of these ideas guided his growth as a science teacher. Two central ideas played a recurring role throughout Tyler's student teaching experience, and each represents conceptions that appeared to remain largely unchanged despite significant activity in other areas of his thinking.

The first concerns Tyler's belief that *conflict is undesirable and ought to be avoided*. Davis, Petish, and Smithey (2006) refer to the "low risk" nature of teaching among many new science teachers, both in terms of activities and classroom management strategies. Tyler's practice exemplified this description. I first noticed his inclination to avoid conflict during an activity when it appeared that even reminding a student to wear safety goggles or tie her hair back around a lit Bunsen burner appeared to be difficult for him.

Another illustration of Tyler's tendency to avoid conflict with students appeared much later in the study. Early on in my visits, I noticed that whenever he was not explicitly at the front of the room talking or giving notes, Tyler always seemed to have students gathering around him. Initially, I wondered if this recurring situation was intentional, having known individual teachers who cultivate helplessness among their students in order to feel needed themselves. When I asked Tyler about seemingly being always surrounded by students, he laughed and said his university supervisor had noticed the same thing. "I think I'm just extremely responsive to the requests of my students, perhaps to a fault." He later added, "Availability is part of my teaching style. It got me on a personal basis with a lot of the students, even the students who weren't always asking questions." Over the course of the study however, I also began to see this practice as a consequence of Tyler's habit of never saying "no" to students, driven by his desire to avoid unnecessary conflict. On reading a draft of this chapter, Tyler confirmed this interpretation. As will be shown, the desire to avoid conflict framed a great deal of Tyler's interactions with students, along with his thinking about the role of race in the science classroom, and perhaps even his pedagogy in general.

The second organizing idea that emerged from the study of Tyler's experience was that *science teaching is primarily the transmission of knowledge from teacher to students*. Tyler was certainly not alone in holding such a conception of teaching. One landmark study of a biology teacher education program described the "transmissionist" views of its teachers as representing a need to "articulate correct scientific knowledge explicitly on the basis of a deep-seated, but uncritically examined, belief that this is what their students would remember" (Hewson, Tabachnick, Zeichner, & Lemberger, 1999, p. 377). This perspective appears to be very common among new science teachers, and stands in contrast to constructivist views about teaching and learning that reject this "transmissionist model" (Bransford et al., 1999; Davis et al., 2006).

This was certainly Tyler's approach, and explains much of what I observed in his classroom. Toward the end of his student teaching semester, I watched Tyler teach a lesson on cellular respiration. He began the class by stating, "I have a PowerPoint presentation, but it would provide you with more information than you need to know. I'm not going to give you too much information." He then launched into a well-prepared, half-hour long lecture on the topic, which he organized in a visually sophisticated way on the whiteboard. Most of the students appeared to be writing in their notebooks as each new slide appeared, but the lecture went uninterrupted by questions from either Tyler or his students. The content of the lesson having been apparently transferred and acquired by students, Tyler concluded the lecture by stating, "Congratulations, you just learned about cellular respiration."

This view of science teaching and learning was undoubtedly linked to Tyler's view of science itself. Although he viewed the practice of science as "posing questions, making observations, trying to solve a problem or answer a question," he also viewed scientific knowledge as "a set body of knowledge." As will be shown, figuring out the extent to which his students had received and understood that set body of knowledge became a central focus of his learning as a physics and biology teacher.

At the beginning of his student teaching, Tyler was very concerned about the possibility that discussions involving race might lead to conflict. In his mind, race was an uncomfortable subject with unpredictable power. When asked how he might respond in my hypothetical Van de Graaff generator scenario, in which a student asks, "This only works on White people's hair, right?" he first tried to think out loud about whether such a belief was true or not, and came to the conclusion that it would probably depend on the individual. When I pressed him on what I would see him do or hear him say if I were an observer, his answer took me by surprise:

> For me actually, I would diffuse it, I wouldn't touch that. I'd say it's a difference in individuals. If I were feeling particularly adventurous, which I don't . . . like I said, the issue of race is especially touchy for me because out of everybody, if anybody's going to get a finger pointed at them for racism, it's a White middle-class male . . . I hate to say it, I'd almost be tempted to sacrifice a little bit of good science to protect myself . . . I don't want to lose my job, quite frankly.

Contrary to Tyler's view of race talk in this example, he was comfortable with the idea of discussing the scientific basis for skin color in his biology class because there were answers that were, in his words, "straightforward and uncontroversial."

He also described how the distribution of skin color among a human population could be represented by a gradient of light to dark with chalk on a chalkboard. In fact, human skin color cannot be accurately represented this way; the expression of the various pigments that make up human skin color are in reality quite complex and remain an area of scientific inquiry (Jablonski, 2006). Such a stance illustrated Tyler's view of scientific knowledge as unproblematic (Smith, Maclin, Houghton, & Hennessey, 2000). In thinking that scientific knowledge in general was more certain than it actually is, he was prone to misrepresenting it in his effort to package it for transmission to students.

But it was the personal threat inherent in certain content that was of greater concern to Tyler. He said that he would be prepared to shut down a discussion on the physiology of skin pigmentation if a student raised ideas about "racial purity" or said something to the effect of "Caucasians are disappearing." To Tyler, such science topics were fraught with danger and could have personal repercussions on his employment as a teacher. He even perceived affirming his race as "White" on a questionnaire as potentially threatening.

There was a parallel line of thinking in Tyler's concern with avoiding conflict in teaching evolution topics. Noting that he had given the matter quite a bit of thought, he said, "I don't necessarily want to get into any trouble with the school board or parents or anybody who happens to disagree with me." Like many biology teachers who are not strong advocates for teaching evolution (Berkman & Plutzer, 2011), Tyler expressed a preference for a focus on micro-evolution, especially if it could be observed in real time, such as the observable resistance of bacteria to antibiotics. He admitted finding macro-evolution tough to understand, "because it's purely theoretical. We [will] never be able to see a time scale of ten million years." To Tyler, it seemed that as long as his teaching was concerned with "straightforward and uncontroversial" facts, he would be safe.

The notion that race talk could have unpredictable consequences had been reinforced for Tyler during his teacher education program at Clayton State. In a course titled Pluralistic Education, his class had discussed Lisa Delpit's widely-read article "The Silenced Dialogue" (1988) in which she argues that minority students must be taught the implicit and explicit rules of the "culture of power" both in schools and in society.

In his written response paper, Tyler made an observation about how his potential criticism of a minority colleague might be perceived as "racially motivated." He had come to the conclusion that in such a case, "I'm going to be called a racist. Even if what I'm saying has some merit to it. It's not an actual discussion, I've simply been shot down, the silenced dialogue." Although Tyler's interpretation of Delpit's article clearly overlooked her main argument, the manner in which his instructor reacted to this paper reinforced his perceptions about the unpredictable power of race talk: "Her response was to give me a zero and call me up after class and sit there and yell at me and call me a racist and tell me that silenced dialogue can only go in one way."

Being called a racist was disturbing for Tyler and did not quite make sense, mostly because he did not see himself in that way. "There's not a racist bone in my body," he told me. In his view racism required malice, and although he noted that such malice might be unconscious to some, he was certain that the "racist" label did not apply to him. The lesson he drew from this incident was that perceptions of racism can be unwarranted, or at the very least may occur as a side effect when a person is not completely mindful or purposeful in his or her actions.

Yet, this is exactly the sort of thinking that is indicative of what King (1991) calls *dysconscious racism*, which she describes as:

> An uncritical habit of mind (including perceptions, attitudes, assumptions, and beliefs) that justifies inequity and exploitation by accepting the existing order of things as given . . . Dysconscious racism is a form of racism that tacitly accepts dominant White norms and privileges. It is not the absence of consciousness (that is, not unconsciousness) but an impaired consciousness or distorted way of thinking about race. (p. 135)

The idea that there could be a sort of inadvertent or collateral discrimination as a result of poor teaching seemed quite plausible to Tyler, but he did not consider it to be racism. Intentions, not consequences, were the determinants of racism to Tyler.

By the end of his student teaching, there was a noticeable change in Tyler's thinking about race as an uncomfortable subject with unpredictable power. Although his conception of racism was still predicated on malicious intent, he seemed less threatened by the prospect of dealing with issues of race in the context of his subject matter. His response to the Van de Graaff question was nearly a complete about-face and was notable in that he had come to see such a question as an opportunity for inquiry with the class:

> It works a little better with straight hair; it doesn't matter whether you're White or Black. If it's nice and straight, beautiful straight strand[s] that can very easily separate from everything else . . . you get a more impressive effect. If you have time, and you have a Black student, ideally one with a giant afro, and a girl with nice long hair, you do the guy with the afro, and you see if there's any sort of difference, see if then you can tie that back to physics and see if you can get them to predict, well why did her hair do that, why did his hair do this? I would say, it works better on straight hair, it's not the issue of White versus Black, it's

. . . Blacker tends to be curlier and be more densely bunched. It doesn't separate out as easily, that's a big difference. If I had time, maybe, you know, I have a day of wiggle room . . . You roll with that experiment. You turn any question you can, if they seem genuinely interested, especially if it's something that you can do right then and there and roll with it.

When I pressed him on his comfort level in conducting such a conversation, remnants of the previous sense of threat still remained. He stated:

You kind of keep an eye on it and make sure it doesn't go somewhere blatantly racist. It kind of depends on the kids' view of this. But I have been nothing but impressed with the kids. Such a diverse school. It strikes me as [if] they're very used to this. Now [if] this is something like the first day and this comes up? That's going to make me uncomfortable. If I've had these kids for a month and I know how they're going to react, I might push this.

Tyler demonstrated a similar change in a scenario posed during the interview in which a hypothetical student asks the question, "How are genes for skin color related to other genes?" In his earlier response, Tyler had said:

Genes are genes. Sometimes they are linked to other genes, sometimes they're not. One instance that we've seen is African Americans tend to be more susceptible to a certain type of heart disease. But for the most part, we share 99.99% of our DNA. These genes do not appear to be linked to anything else apart from melanin production.

Revisiting this question at the end of student teaching, Tyler offered a specific and detailed example of how the gene for sickle-cell anemia is common in African Americans yet also confers some resistance to malaria. Like many preservice biology teachers I have known, his conceptions regarding genes seem to relate solely to those that give rise to visible traits, but he does not shrink from this conversation. It also appeared that a better understanding of his subject matter, as indicated by his greater facility with discussing science content than shown previously, had influenced his responses to the Van De Graaff as well as the linked-gene questions.

Two conceptions in particular seemed more plausible to Tyler at the end of his student teaching than they had at the start. The first concerned Tyler's initial conception of race as an uncomfortable subject with unpredictable power. Tyler's sense of this threat became more nuanced over the semester, beginning with his early observation that, at least at Central High, "everybody just treats everybody else absolutely equal." Over time, he began to perceive that race is a non-issue in this school, perhaps reflecting an overly optimistic view of the salience of race at Central. He observed an absence of self-segregation in his classes, which he had expected to see, and remarked on the casual way students deployed race for humor.

He recounted an incident when a quiz buzzer failed to light for an African American student during a test review competition because he had not been the first to press the button to answer. The student asked, "Is it because I'm Black?" to the reported amusement of the whole class. This occurrence was reassuring to Tyler because it was more proof to him that race was not a big deal in his school.

Tyler was aware of racial disparities in Central High School's graduation rates; in the year prior, the high school completion rate at Central High had been 89% for White students, compared with 70% for Black students and 45% for Hispanic students. He also observed the racialized nature of academic tracking that led to a disproportionate number of White students taking advanced science electives, including the anatomy and physiology classes he co-taught. Tyler was uncertain exactly how these situations had come about, though he did recognize the difficulty students faced if they wished to break out of the lower track. The conception that *race is connected to the structure of the school* had also become intelligible to Tyler in a way that it previously had not been.

Tyler's practice also revolved heavily around grades, as both a motivation for student learning and an outcome measure. Ironically, he described his coursework in assessment at Clayton State as "irrelevant" because of the course's focus on holistic assessment. This was incompatible with Tyler's view of science subject matter:

> All they stressed in the assessment course was holistic, holistic, holistic, which is great for some subjects. Science is a set body of knowledge. I guess they were a little wishy-washy for me. They always wanted a rubric. They always wanted multiple assessment strategies. And I realize the old cut-and-dried "Here is a worksheet, do the worksheet" is overused, but at the same time, it's a useful tool. And it gets some extended practice out there.

For Tyler, assessment was the act of producing grades—what is sometimes called *summative* assessment. This contrasts with *formative* assessment, which is the act of figuring out what students already know for the purpose of guiding instruction and providing students with feedback on their thinking. Black and Wiliam (1998) conducted a review of all the studies done on the effects of formative assessment practices and found it to be one of the strongest educational interventions in existence. The use of formative assessment practices however, did not fit well with Tyler's view of teaching and learning.

From a transmissionist perspective, eliciting a student's prior knowledge and providing targeted feedback may hold value as classroom actions but they do little to measure the extent to which knowledge has been successfully delivered to the intended recipient. Simply put, Tyler did not consider these practices as assessment, and tools like holistic rubrics were just distractions from the straight-forward task of assigning a grade.

In a tangible sense, the pursuit of justifiable grades seemed to be a defining feature of Tyler's practice and did not change appreciably during the study. However, he did begin to recognize and question the fact that the grades he assigned for lower achieving students often represented literacy or organizational skills, and were not always valid appraisals of knowledge. By the end of his student teaching, this focus on grades led Tyler to a categorical observation about his students that invoked race:

> I've noticed that the only thing race really tended to dictate—and this certainly wasn't a truism, but it was slightly more than average—African American students tended to have slightly poorer writing skills. It wasn't that they couldn't get their ideas across—they tended to [be] much stronger in analogies, but actually writing a sound scientific sentence? . . . That didn't fly a lot. I don't even want to say a lot, but more often than not.

The implication for Tyler was that he had to scrutinize written student responses more closely when assigning grades, because student writing did not always reflect what students had actually learned:

> When you look at the answer . . . for a problem, you can't just literally see "Is this right? Is this wrong?" you have to figure out what they meant. And often times they were correct, they were absolutely correct, they got the idea, they just didn't know how to put pen to paper and express the idea in a classroom setting. And that was very quickly a realization; I cannot grade this right or wrong. I need to figure out what they were trying to say. I need to read between the lines.

Though it appeared he was struggling for the right words, Tyler spoke in terms that he would have likely found threatening at the start of the year. Anticipating the effect a student's race might have on particular learning behaviors still felt like stereotyping to him, as he noted:

> It's never fair to hold somebody to a stereotype, but odds are stereotypes have come about for a reason, so be aware of them, but . . . don't even really let them guide you. Know that they're there and be aware . . . use it as something to look for.

Clearly, Tyler was searching for a way to generalize about categories of students without resorting to stereotypes. In the language of conceptual change, he had become dissatisfied with the explanatory power of stereotypes. It seems likely that a better understanding of cultural patterns of communication may offer both a better explanation for his observations and suggestions for leveraging this knowledge for deeper student learning.

⌷

Tyler's apparent change in his comfort level with race talk paralleled a change in his overall level of comfort in the classroom, though his pedagogy did not appreciably change during the semester of student teaching. There is direct evidence of Tyler's growth in his content knowledge over time. In September, he clearly conflated plant respiration and photosynthesis: "[When] plants respire . . . they use carbon dioxide instead of oxygen." This is incorrect. The process of respiration in plants uses oxygen, just like in humans. Photosynthesis, on the other hand uses carbon dioxide and releases oxygen into the air.

In January, his understanding of cellular respiration was significantly improved, and he discussed that student misconceptions arose because "every science course from third grade on taught you that we [humans] breathe, plants do photosynthesis."

Interestingly, he did not seem to consider this improved understanding an act of learning on his part: "I don't think [my content knowledge] has improved, I think I've kind of had to straighten out some understandings, get it a little reclassified. It's different . . . having the knowledge, and then having it wonderfully put in a row and ordered, and ready for dissemination to everybody else."

For Tyler, learning was an act of knowledge acquisition, as opposed to a process of knowledge construction, a belief clearly enacted in his pedagogy. There were a number of times in the biology class when he described what was going on (either to the students or to me) as "providing information." He often used phrases that described how information-rich a given topic was, followed by the reassurance that they would not necessarily need to "cover it all."

It is clear from the data that Tyler viewed his own teaching as the act of making sure his students "had the knowledge." Subsequently, his observations of his African American students' writing challenges indicated the existence of a communication barrier between information flowing from student to teacher. The notion that such barriers might exist going in the other direction did not arise in our conversations, though such an insight did appear in a reflection he wrote regarding feedback he had received from his students on his use of the phrase "common sense." He concluded that using the phrase was "demeaning and discouraging to any student that doesn't already possess the prior knowledge."

When I asked Tyler if his observation about his African American students' strengths in making analogies had any implications for his teaching, he replied, "I didn't really change my teaching too much because naturally, [making analogies] is my strength." Rather than interpreting his students' facility with analogies as a resource to be tapped further, Tyler viewed his insight as a way to confirm that the transmission of content from teacher to student had been accomplished.

Tyler found it difficult to incorporate the contributions of his students into his teaching, despite a strongly espoused desire to do so. Two instances of student-teacher interactions I observed support this assertion and also illuminated Tyler's understanding about the role of student prior knowledge and conceptions in the learning process.

In the first instance, an African American student (whom I had identified as a diligent note-taker) raised his hand during one of Tyler's lectures on cellular respiration to say that he had seen a Discovery Channel episode on running, and that they had talked about how runners learn to breathe without getting tired. Tyler's response to this observation was to try to explain it, stating, "Maybe they're somehow training their mitochondria to do that." As he continued the lecture, it occurred to me that an opportunity to capitalize on this student's interest, or use such knowledge as a conceptual peg on which to build understanding, had been missed.

In another interaction, Tyler made an announcement to his biology class: "Just so I know, we have an upcoming lab and I wanted to ask, is anybody here allergic to peanuts?" No one acknowledged an allergy, but one African American student asked "What kind of peanuts?" Tyler seemed to interpret this as a wise-crack and responded to her with exasperation, "What do you mean what kind of peanuts?" When she asked, rather seriously, "Are they sunflower seeds?" the possibility occurred to me that this student may have placed all sorts of nuts and seeds under her own personal conception of "peanuts," and that Tyler's conception of peanuts was probably very different from hers. He appeared somewhat annoyed and got more specific, responding, "They're just regular Planters roasted peanuts." The student did not press the matter beyond this answer, for Tyler's tone was definitive. Still, the incident left me with the impression that had Tyler been in the habit of carefully probing his students' thinking, he might have learned something very interesting in this exchange. His fleeting perception of a young girl's foolishness and sass—perhaps even misbehavior—might have been transformed momentarily into a snapshot of her inner world, useful for charting future paths of teaching and learning.

Having finished his program at the end of the fall semester, Tyler was now in the unenviable position of having to look for a job in the middle of the school year, when most area schools had stopped accepting applications for substitutes, let alone full-time teachers. In the spring, we met in a coffee shop to discuss the draft of his case, which I had emailed to him in advance. Neither of us was in any particular hurry that day, and we talked for hours.

"My impression?" he asked when I inquired how well he felt the case represented his experiences. "It's pretty close. It was interesting to read someone else's take on this, having lived it."

One thing we discussed that afternoon was how Tyler's perceptions about the role of race changed over the course of the semester. I pointed out to him how, in his later interview, he used terms like "nice," "beautiful," and "impressive," and positive phrasing such as "easily separates," and "better" when describing White hair. In his description of Black hair however, he used terms like "dense," "giant," and "bunched" and negative phrasing like "doesn't separate." He was genuinely intrigued by this observation, and admitted being unaware of his use of language in this way. He remarked that a recent interest in psychology had led him to read more about how the brain worked, and he made the observation that perhaps he had somehow been "primed to use" such terms unconsciously.

This was the first evidence I obtained that suggested Tyler might be coming to view racism as something other than willful discrimination, and he appeared less threatened than he might have been earlier had he been confronted with evidence that conflicted with his view of himself as not racist. Nevertheless, it probably didn't hurt that it was me—a fellow White guy with no power over his job prospects—pointing it out to him.

CHAPTER 3

Navigating Dilemmas of Sinking and Swimming

Corrine—Biology, General Science

> I don't think I could have been a teacher without having been a mom. I didn't have the patience for it when I was twenty-two. I know kids need that patience, they need that time, they need your attention, and I wasn't willing to give it at that point in time. I didn't realize how much I was willing to give kids until after I became a mom.
>
> —Corrine

Just before her high school juniors and seniors enter the room, Corrine shares her lesson plan with me. "I'll be essentially just telling them what's on the test so they can study," she confides, "but they won't." Her anatomy and physiology students soon stream into the room from lunch, many discussing plans for the upcoming 4-day weekend. One student drops his bag and heads straight to the front of the room to show Corrine his chest X-ray from a recent hospital visit. She examines the acetate enthusiastically, pointing at different structures and questioning him about his diagnosis before returning it.

Class begins at 11:25 AM, and at the bell Corrine says, "Okay, ladies and gentlemen, we have a few things to do today." As conversations draw to a close she adds, "It shouldn't take too long, so you'll have time to socialize and finish your other work later." This group is about half the size of her freshman environmental science classes and presents significantly fewer classroom management challenges.

She begins walking through the aisles of single desks, which are arranged in rows and columns facing forward. "I'm handing back your senses packet," she says. One student's backpack is on the floor and Corrine trips over it. She catches her balance and does not fall, but is clearly in pain. "That was not good," she says, holding her knee up slightly. The owner of the bag apologizes and moves his bag.

"I'll try not to cry," Corrine says with a wincing smile. She maintains a brave face as she limps through the distribution of the remaining packets, which students leaf through purposefully as she slides into the chair at the front desk.

"On the test," she says from the chair, "be very precise in your answers." A student walks in late. "Nice of you to join us," Corrine says to him. Another student gives him a hard time, asking him where his pass is, but Corrine is continuing with the review. She points to some specific examples in the packet she has just returned. "Be careful of the question," she continues. "And answer the question that is asked." Corrine reads through the list projected on the board: "Nervous system review: 70 points total, 20 anatomy lab practical, 32 on Scantron—bring #2 pencil—18 points short answer."

The next slide, labeled "Neurons," details the exact content the students will need to know for the test one week from today. Corrine reads the slide to the students. "Be able to name the parts of a neuron and the function of these parts." The presentation aligns with the packet and students ask questions along the way, apparently correcting their work. "Be able to name the different types of neurons and what they do," she adds.

"We get a note card, right?" a student in the center of the class asks. Corrine nods and reminds them that it must be a standard-sized note card and may contain notes only on physiology, not anatomy. She then advances to a slide about the brain and the various functions of the central and peripheral nervous systems. While she is describing the autonomic nervous system, a student calls out, "How's your knee?" Corrine laughs, saying it's better, and jokes with the students that they ought to be able to explain the neurological basis for her knee pain on the upcoming test.

Corrine continues the review. "What is the function of cerebrospinal fluid?" she asks as the next slide appears. The class is now quiet, and only two students still write in their packets while the rest of the class just looks at the screen. She advances to a slide labeled "Senses." In discussing what students need to know about the ear, she asks, "Do you want me to take out the model?" The students are unresponsive, and Corrine waits patiently.

One student breaks the silence to ask, "Are we ever going to finish those video things?"

"No. Well . . ." Corrine considers this for a moment. "We might actually have some time today." She then proceeds to the final slide, which details what students need to know about the myelination of neurons.

"Okay, that's it," she says; the test review has taken a total of 15 minutes. "We have some time," she says. "I'd like you to finish up the reflex lab if you haven't already." She reminds students of other ways they can use class time to study for the test. As students begin their work, one asks where Corrine's cooperating teacher, Mrs. Mueller, is today. Corrine answers that she is in and out of the building, planting trees with school groups for Earth Day.

Most students form study groups; a few work independently. One group asks Corrine for the plastic model of the ear. She pulls it off the top shelf, and brings the eye model down as well. The students in the group ask her to help with the ear physiology review, and a question about the cochlea sends all of them, including Corrine, to the textbook.

Corrine notices two students playing with the electronic whiteboard. She calls across the room, "Only with permission." They put the markers down and return to the lab table, where another group is using a flashlight and ruler to examine the dilation of each other's pupils. This task soon complete, the group sits around and talks while Corrine enters information at the front computer. Two girls approach Corrine and ask her to set up the video on neurological disorders so they can finish watching it. One segment of the video is about a man diagnosed with aphasia, who speaks nonsense words as if they were clear speech, and it captures the attention of the whole class. "What's wrong with him?" asks one student from the back of the room. Corrine responds, "Look in your packet."

At noon, there are only a few minutes left in the period, and with the video over, all of the students are sitting and talking, either on top of the lab tables or at their desks. Corrine is still at the computer and delicately taunts the class, "So you all have plenty of time to study, right? Because you could be studying right now." As students congregate by the door, she calls out, "I'm expecting some really good grades on Wednesday," before wishing them a happy weekend.

📋

Corrine grew up in the Midwestern United States in what she described as a "very White, fairly poor, rural background." Despite coming of age in what she dubbed the "lecture, problems, and canned lab" era of high school science, biology held a lifelong fascination for her. As a college student, she quickly decided on a career in science, and thrived as a learner in the university environment. "I soak up lecture like you would not believe," she told me.

After receiving her PhD in molecular genetics from Delorenzo University, Corrine pursued her desire to teach by working with undergraduates in a university research environment. Though she maintained a love of molecular biology, she found the actual day-to-day work of a research scientist uninspiring. A history teacher friend helped her make arrangements to spend a day in his school's biology and chemistry classes, and this experience catalyzed Corrine's decision to become a high school science teacher.

Shortly after her youngest child was of preschool age, Corrine applied to the post-baccalaureate program at Acacia College, a private institution in Delorenzo City affiliated with the Catholic Church. Like the other programs in this study, the initial semester consisted of on-campus coursework. In each subsequent term, prospective teachers spent more time in schools, through the final semester when full-time student teaching took place.

As a program requirement in the spring of her second semester, Corrine spent time in an area middle school observing classes. Her impressions described in a reflection paper for her Human Issues class are worth quoting at length:

> I walked into [my initial practicum] middle school on Thursday and was quite shocked. I live in the neighborhood and know that the student population is mixed in our school, but I was not prepared for the numbers. Maybe one-third of the class was White, maybe. I was assigned my group of mentees and we went out in the hall to chat. I had no idea what to say to these kids so we went over the basics. What do you like to do? What's your family like? What are you interested in? They are neat kids but I don't know how to form a connection with them. I'm a little worried that I'm going to be the "weird White lady we have to hang around with." What it comes down to is fear. I am afraid. What if I make a mistake and insult these kids or make them feel inferior or anger their parent(s)? I am completely ignorant of the cultural background of these children. We are not peers. How can I make a connection with these kids and get comfortable enough to teach them? It is a little about race, since that is part of their identity but my issue is really with their culture. I am completely out of my element. I live "in the city" now but I'm not a part of minority urban culture.

Later, she described this first encounter with diversity in her middle school practicum as "one of the most enlightening experiences of my whole program, and the hardest thing to deal with."

Corrine's second practicum placement, which occurred in the fall semester during this study, was at Acacia High School, the K–12 private school associated with Acacia College. Though her role in the class was primarily observational, she did have some opportunities to teach lessons.

Going into full-time student teaching, Corrine's goals included learning to plan coherent and differentiated lessons, becoming more comfortable in the classroom, and learning "those little efficiency things to keep a classroom rolling." Classroom management issues had been important to Corrine during practicum, but she did not see maintaining control of student behavior as an end in itself. She was wary of creating "a false atmosphere of an efficient classroom, where students are doing what they are supposed to do rather than really learning and engaging in the curriculum."

Corrine's full-time student teaching placement was at Ridgefield High School, in a rural suburb ten miles south of Delorenzo City. The local Chamber of Commerce described the town in one of their publications as "a family-friendly, small-town atmosphere with easy access to all that nearby [Delorenzo City] has to offer: world-class education, employment, and cultural affairs opportunities." As shown in Table 3.1, nearly 95% of the students in the school identified as White.

Her cooperating teacher, Mrs. Mueller, had been certified 5 years prior by the National Board for Professional Teaching Standards, and was one of only 30 board-certified teachers in her state with the Early Adolescent/Science certification. Corrine quickly assumed responsibility for a Human Anatomy and Physiology class for 11th- and 12th-grade students, and two sections of environmental science, a required course for all 9th graders in the school.

The Ridgefield environmental science curriculum was part of a coordinated departmental effort to focus on outcome-based education (e.g., Spady, 1994), in which units and lessons were aligned with identified student learning outcomes across the 4 years of science courses offered by the school. Therefore, much of the curriculum had already been planned in detail. Initially, Mrs. Mueller taught the morning section of the class, and Corrine used the same lesson plans with her afternoon students, a practice called "follow teaching" within the teacher education programs of this study. And though by mid-April Corrine had assumed responsibility for all five of her cooperating teachers' classes, she was expected by Mrs. Mueller to draw heavily on the curriculum materials previously developed for each course. This left precious little space for Corrine's creativity as an ambitious student teacher. However, a number of her students had individual education plans (IEPs), and Corrine worked with special education assistants to modify her lessons throughout the semester.

One of the notable features of Corrine's placement at Ridgefield was the extent to which technology was incorporated into the ongoing activities of the class. Mrs. Mueller maintained an extensive website for her courses that included lesson notes, slide presentations, class assignments, project details, and additional resources. Student grades were kept in an online database, and student assignments were submitted through a plagiarism prevention website. One of the effects of this arrangement was that both Corrine and her cooperating teacher spent substantial amounts of classroom time at the teacher computer workstation in the front of the room. Another was the unmistakable message that the availability of these resources placed the responsibility for learning squarely on the shoulders of students.

In such an atmosphere, taking responsibility for one's own learning appeared to be the central message to students and the student teacher alike. Corrine

Table 3.1. Enrollment and Race/Ethnicity Data for Corrine's Student Teaching Placement at Ridgefield High School

Total Enrollment	American Indian	Asian	Black	Hispanic	White
1,225	0.2%	1.3%	1.8%	2.1%	94.5%

reported that her cooperating teacher's attitude toward teaching juniors and seniors was "sink-or-swim," and I often felt during observations that Mrs. Mueller had adopted the same attitude toward Corrine as a student teacher, though she was certainly generous in terms of providing resources. Mrs. Mueller often left the room while Corrine was teaching, and Corrine reported receiving little feedback from Mrs. Mueller and her university supervisor. When she did, it was generally positive but nonspecific.

⬚

I followed Corrine for the second year of her teacher education program at Acacia College, and it quickly became clear to me that many of her conceptions had already been undergoing change as a result of her first year of coursework and fieldwork. In our initial interview I presented her with a common survey question on race and ethnicity and asked her to describe her thoughts about it.[1] Corrine felt that such data ought to be used ethically, but remained uncertain as to why someone's identity mattered:

> It really shouldn't matter what your background is . . . I mean you can have an African American person who grew up in a middle-class rich suburb that has the same experience as all their White colleagues, pretty much. And then you can have a White person who grew up in the trailer park on the other side of the tracks who has a very different view. So it really shouldn't matter. And yet I know that, statistically, different populations don't do as well on different tests. And why is that?

Though Corrine understood the multiple ways "diversity" could be interpreted, she also recognized that there was something missing from her perspective. Specifically, her mental model of the way diversity operated in education could not account for differential levels of academic achievement across racial groups.

When discussing culture in our first interview, Corrine described culture as something that is part of someone's "upbringing" and influences individuals' ideas about what is and is not appropriate. In a later interview, she drew on her family history to describe how she perceived the distinctions between biology, race, and culture:

> I have siblings who are Korean. I'm not Korean, but they're my siblings. Culturally, they're Norwegian, you know? They're not really culturally Korean. They did not grow up in the Korean culture. They grew up here in America, so they're American and they have more Norwegian and Swedish traditions than they do Korean traditions. So culturally, they're not Korean. Genetically,

they're Korean. Racially, they're Korean. If you look at them, you would think that they're Asian, not Norwegian. If you read a description of their family life, you would think that they are Norwegian, not Korean. So that's what I mean by cultural versus genetic, or biological.

In talking about the role of culture in schooling, Corrine included attitudes toward school and responses to authority. She saw this view of culture as useful for identifying and solving problems, but early on did not portray it as a resource to be tapped or as way to think about student learning.

Corrine also felt that culture played a role in the value that African American and Latino students and their families placed on education. She said that she had encountered this idea in an education journal prior to becoming a teacher, though neither of us could identify the actual article. Even after a year of student teaching, she did not appear to recognize that such judgments about the value of education are notoriously unreliable, particularly when made by White teachers of children of color in urban environments (Compton-Lilly, 2003). This example also highlights a difficulty faced by many prospective teachers, White and non-White alike, in talking about student diversity in categorical terms (Paine, 1990). Corrine's desire to make observations appeared to come into conflict with her unwillingness to be perceived as employing a stereotype.

However, she did express an awareness of systemic racial discrimination, and credited her Human Issues course with challenging her previous ideas on this topic. During this course, she reported changing her thinking about the meaning of racism and the implications of benefiting from privilege:

> When you come from a system of privilege and even if you're aware of the issues and don't think that you're part of the problem, it's really hard not to be part of the problem, because you benefit from the system. . . . It's also hard to admit that you're racist.

Corrine had also come to recognize that part of the work of teachers was to be proactive against discrimination:

> If you're not addressing the specific needs of the student, you're doing them a disservice, and whether that's a part of their skin color or not, or whether they're learning disabled or non-learning disabled, if you're not taking that into account, you're discriminating against them.

Unlike some of the other study participants, she viewed the absence of malice and the presence of discrimination as two distinct issues. This perspective allowed Corrine to assume responsibility for being explicitly anti-discriminatory in her practice, and contributed to the unsettling feelings she had experienced in her middle school observations:

This is something that's been hard for me to think about. We just had a class on it—if you're not a part of the solution, you're a part of the problem. If you benefit from a system that's racially biased, you can't really separate yourself outside of that one hundred percent. You can be aware of it, and you can try and counteract it, but if you're not doing something to counteract it, you're participating in this racially biased system, and therefore you are practicing racism.

What it actually looks like for a teacher to counteract the racially biased system she described, to move beyond mindfulness into action, was still unknown to Corrine as she began her practicum semester. As I show below, without someone to help her enact these ideas in her daily practice, Corrine's growth in this area remained limited, even as her desire to be "part of the solution" remained strong.

Corrine's conceptions about the pedagogical implications of student diversity underwent only minor changes during the year-long time frame of this study, and it is difficult to avoid the conclusion that this was a result of the limited of racial, ethnic, and cultural diversity in her fieldwork placements. The student bodies in her third-semester practicum and full-time student teaching placements were primarily White and middle- to upper-class, and this demographic homogeneity appeared to influence how she framed the problems of teaching and learning in her classes.

During the winter break between practicum and student teaching, Corrine fulfilled a state teacher education requirement by taking a course in Native American Studies offered by the State University Extension. It was at this time I asked for her response to a hypothetical scenario involving Native American students, whom other teachers had identified as "shy" because they did not participate in classroom discussions. In her response, she readily invoked the notion of culture for an explanation:

> From literature it's actually . . . Native Americans are taught not to look at teachers, and so that may be of the appearance of shy[ness], but they're actually taught to question. That's part of their culture, so you'd have to understand the culture.

Though she generalized Native American culture as unified and undifferentiated rather than as a diverse set of groups with a broad range of cultural beliefs and practices (Lomawaima, 1995), she clearly viewed culture as a mediating factor that determines how students experience school. When asked how she might approach such a situation as a teacher, Corrine also recognized the logic of structuring her classroom in ways that were consistent with her Native American students' culture:

Because community discussion and community voice is very common in their culture, I'd probably try and go to group discussion and participate in that, and encourage that instead of calling on students, and try to get more discussion going. That way they can ask questions in a culturally appropriate manner for them, and still learn, still participate without being sort of seen as aggressive in their culture.

Such an idea is consistent with certain teacher-student communication strategies advocated by multicultural education scholars (e.g., Gay, 2002; Lee, 2007). Though the Native American Studies course did not address pedagogy, Corrine pointed to it as the source of her idea.

In the months to come, Corrine did not have any opportunities to expand or explore this notion of cultural congruence in communication patterns during her student teaching experience with primarily White students. At the end of her program, 5 months after completing the Native American Studies course, she echoed her earlier observation about cultural practices, but her preferred approach to this situation no longer involved ensuring culturally congruent forms of communication. Rather, she viewed this scenario in terms of ensuring comfort and an equal opportunity to speak in low-threat situations, without being put "on the spot."

Give them an opportunity to speak to share their information in turn. After you've done your spiel, you may say to a student: "So-and-so, do you have anything you want to add or comment on, or any questions?" So basically, you pass the floor over to that person, and that can be done with any student. If you do that on a regular basis with a variety of people, you're not singling anybody out and you're giving the opportunity for everyone to participate.

Culture still offered Corrine a set of ideas to explain student behavior, yet a more general management strategy designed to ensure students' comfort and motivation for participation had taken precedence over her previous idea that culture represented a pedagogical resource.

During the second and third interviews, Corrine also identified a number of instances when she felt that she was not understood by her students. The underlying conception that she formed out of these observations was: *The way in which a teacher communicates with her students can negatively affect student learning.* Corrine recognized that some sort of blockage existed between her delivery of information and her students' reception of it. Though she did not portray these blockages as cultural in nature, such a conception may blaze a trail for Corrine's future professional growth. An ability to identify cultural differences in students' communication and participation styles is a prerequisite for being able to incorporate such understandings into one's teaching.

Responding to a draft of this case, Corrine stated that she still wished to employ culturally familiar patterns of interactions with her students, even though that had not been her answer at the time. She recognized that her answer had been largely a reflection of her situation in Ridgefield, but wanted me to understand that she had not forgotten her earlier response.

📋

Just before student teaching, I reminded Corrine about her earlier struggle with understanding the relationship between academic achievement and race, and she told me that she was now considering this issue as a matter of teacher expectations:

It's expectations, right? If you're expecting the White students to perform at this [higher] level and you expect the Black or non-White students to perform at this [lower] level they [will] meet those expectations. . . . Basically if you don't do something actively to bridge that gap it's not going to happen.

Corrine had clearly made the connection between expectations and achievement, and even expressed her responsibility as a teacher to address the problem of lowered expectations for non-White students. In the sink-or-swim environment of her student teaching placement, however, acting on this awareness was easier said than done. As I detail below, by aiming to keep her academic expectations high, Corrine's choices in the following episode paradoxically served to further marginalize one of her few students of color.

I visited Corrine's classroom on a regular basis, and by mid-March she had clearly established herself as the sole teacher in the afternoon Environmental Science class. On my arrival, it was clear that Corrine had been playing defense with a number of students who disputed their third-marking-period grades. "I'm having empathy problems," she told me as an aside after she had sent them all back to their seats to begin the lesson.

Later that period, as most students worked independently at their seats, I watched Corrine interact with Martin, one of two African American students in the class. As a 10th-grader, Martin was a year older than most of the other students. He had transferred earlier in the year from another district, where Environmental Science had not been a required 9th-grade course, and he was in the position of needing to catch up on the material he had missed.

Martin and Corrine discussed the failing grade of 58% he had received on a recent project, which left him a few points shy of passing the class for the marking period. Corrine presented him with a number of options, indicating that any of them would bring his grade above passing. I was intrigued in the way this discussion focused on completing academic requirements, with no discussion at all about the content or Martin's understanding of it. By the end of the conversation, Martin appeared disappointed, and it seemed to me—and perhaps to him also—that there would not be enough time for him to complete any of the options before the deadline the following day. Corrine drew on the sink-or-swim metaphor to describe Martin's academic difficulties to me: "He's a sophomore in a freshman class and is really behind, totally underwater."

Corrine's conceptions about what it meant to hold high academic expectations implied holding Martin accountable for meeting the same standards as everyone else, which in her cooperating teacher's class meant the completion of required assignments. Corrine was choosing what she felt was the right way to help Martin, and that to accord him extra attention would have represented lowering her expectations of what he was able to accomplish on his own.

After reading a draft of this account, Corrine framed the problem differently, invoking one of the central dilemmas in her practice: the need to give grades. Acknowledging that Martin's passing test scores showed that he apparently understood the material, she noted that he "wasn't doing the other things" needed to pass. Corrine compared Martin to a White student who was in a similar situation. This student had completed none of the other work, but had received much higher grades on his tests, bringing his final grade above passing. Corrine explained:

> I hate the whole grading process, and wish we could just get rid of grades. But it's not just the knowledge they need; it's the work ethic and skills. How are they going to go on in life if they can't do these skills?

A teacher in the resource room to which Martin had been assigned for one period each day shared some additional information with Corrine that changed the way she thought about Martin's work ethic and skills. This teacher reported that Martin had taken it on himself to tutor a number of the other African American students also assigned to the resource room. In fact, he had apparently been helping other students at the expense of time that he could have spent on his own work. Though Corrine recognized that this information helped to explain why Martin had not completed his work, as a student teacher she felt compelled to stick with her cooperating teacher's grading system. Corrine suspected that race somehow played a role in this situation, but she was not certain how to characterize what that role might be.

Among many marginalized groups in the modern world, a collective approach to knowledge is strongly valued (Ladson-Billings, 2000; Roth & Lee, 2002), and achievement is recognized with respect to the wider group. The help Martin provided to his fellow students certainly represented "work ethic and skills" for which he could have been given credit, yet to do so would have undoubtedly clashed with the rigid framework and underlying individualistic rationale for the system of curriculum and grades in Corrine's school. Corrine's high expectations in this example appeared to backfire into a pedagogy of exclusion (Mitakidou, Tressou, Swadener, & Grant, 2009), ultimately exacerbating the racial academic achievement gap she had earlier decried.

My interpretation is that the same rigid structure that labeled Martin as a failing student also coerced Corrine into acting against her more humanistic impulses. This raises the question of how much we ought to expect student teachers to push for change in an environment where doing so would clearly lead to conflict with established norms. I think of Jonathan Kozol's (2007) counsel for teachers to act as witnesses to injustice and to have the moral courage to do so. "The teachers for whom I feel the greatest sadness," he says, "are the ones who choke on their beliefs, who never act on their ideals, who never know the taste of struggle in a decent cause and never know the thrill of even partial victories." (p. 193).

The real question may be whether or not teachers are being prepared in ways that allow them to bear witness to injustice and even act under hazard of professional and personal consequences. My own opinion is that we desperately need teachers who will confront inane bureaucratic practices when necessary and take the kind of risks that would have privileged a humane response to Martin. Cultivating the necessary combination of fearlessness and pragmatism seems to me a worthy goal for teacher preparation.

📋

At the beginning of the study, I asked Corrine to examine some pages from a widely-used high school biology textbook. One page from an early chapter discussed the physiology of skin, including the role of melanin as a skin pigment that absorbs various wavelengths of light. A page from a later chapter used an unsourced—and in my view, questionably constructed—graph to demonstrate the fact that human skin color was determined by multiple genes. Corrine noted that the section that portrayed melanin production in human skin as a response to sunlight did not align well with the later genetic explanation for skin color and suggested alternate presentations to bring the two ideas together in a more meaningful way. In this discussion, Corrine focused primarily on thinking about ways for her students to understand the content.

When I asked her if the racial or ethnic composition of her class could have any implications for the lesson on skin color variations, it was difficult for her to make sense of the question. She pointed at the textbook graph and said:

> This is a statement of fact, it's no judgment on worth or expectations. I mean, if anything, people with the darkest and the lightest skin are the exceptions

rather than the rule, and it's an issue of do you apprize the exception or do you apprize the mean? You know? And that has absolutely no place in a science classroom. This is a statement of evaluation—it has no judgment as to worth.

In Corrine's view, taking note of her students' skin color was inextricably linked to value judgments—something to be avoided at all costs. However, content that represented statements of fact were in themselves unproblematic. Corrine and I later discussed this point at length, and she clarified her thinking at the time for me. She said that though the diversity of her class might have influenced her teaching, she "probably would have tried not to go there for fear of upsetting folks . . . of being perceived as insensitive."

Though Corrine held firm to the conception that *scientific data is impersonal, even when race is part of the science content,* she no longer believed that race was irrelevant to science content. In both the second and third interviews, Corrine explained that variations in skin tones among the students presented an opportunity to demonstrate how sample size affected the construction of a graph. She discussed how she would collect data on students' skin tones and described why such an activity was unproblematic in her view:

> I'm assuming that there would be some sort of a chart that goes along with this classification. . . . So everybody could match their skin tone and put the data up, on a smartboard in this case, and just draw our curve in class. . . . For me, genetics is just science. . . . It's the context. If you were talking about skin color in a social science class, that can have a different connotation than in a science class. I mean, if you're talking about genetics or anatomy, that has nothing to do with social conditions, it has to do with your DNA.

When I pressed her, Corrine said that she would do such an activity even if she only had a single student of color in the class, citing her responsibility for creating a safe classroom environment. When I asked if anything would make her decide that such an activity was not safe to do, she maintained her view on the impersonal nature of scientific data, but took other factors into account as well:

> Part of that would be the climate of the school, or if there was some serious tensions with particular students. Even then I would hope that with the community building that we've done at the beginning, the climate of the classroom would be such that the students would know that this is not a judgment of them as an individual or them as a person of a specific culture or community—that we're talking about data. And data should be impersonal. There isn't necessarily a good or a bad. It's data. There's accurate data; there's inaccurate data.

For Corrine, what students brought to a discussion about the biology of skin color was limited to their skin itself. Clearly, she was viewing her students as a resource in a way she previously had not. However, she did not yet see a role for her students' prior ideas about skin color and life experiences as an influence in their learning of science content. Her scientific perspective on the genetic basis and physical makeup of skin and skin color—clearly influenced by her previous PhD work in genetics—led her to approach the topic in a straightforward manner, without consideration of the conceptual resources—helpful or otherwise—that her students would bring to this task.

Race is often noticed in academic contexts for students of color in ways that it is not for White students (G. L. Thompson, 2004), and this has consequences for both academic achievement and identity development (Steele, 2010; Tatum, 2003). Yet it is also true that schools commonly reproduce social inequalities while portraying such inequalities as fair and natural (Villegas & Lucas, 2002). Failure to acknowledge race, or attend to race as having pedagogical implications, can negatively impact student learning (Ladson-Billings, 1994; Paley, 1989; Zeichner, 1996). As much as Corrine might wish her students' racial "data" to be impersonal, it never is.

◻

When Corrine referred to a lesson on the genetic basis of human skin color as "just science" and "impersonal facts," she was also representing her conceptions about scientific knowledge and her conceptions about science learning. Her reliance on delivering information to students, such as in using PowerPoint slides to accompany her lectures, would suggest Corrine's teaching was largely transmissionist in nature. Yet she later told me that her frequent use of PowerPoint was a limitation imposed by her cooperating teacher, and that she would have much preferred teaching in a different way.

What changed during her teacher education program was not her idea that teaching consisted of giving facts to students, but that *in order for it to be considered learning, the students had to do something with those facts.* When asked in the initial interview if a nature show on television could be considered an example of teaching biology to a student viewer at home, she focused primarily on the transmission of information to the student:

> Whoever made the program, they're providing information. That is an aspect of teaching . . . . The student is choosing to view it, so in essence is teaching themselves, but whoever put it together is providing information for that student. So that's information transfer . . . I would say yes, because the people that made it think that there is some value in the information that they're disseminating.

By the third interview, Corrine had recognized that disseminating information alone was not enough to ensure learning. There had to be some activity on the
part of the student, preferably through guided directives:

> There may be learning going on there, [but] I'm not necessarily sure that there
> would be teaching going on without some sort of directive to the student
> about things to look for, questions to think about, something like that. . . .
> You need to do something with that information in order for me to consider
> it teaching. It might be learning, and it might be a good way to augment your
> teaching but . . . [I'm] not so sure if I would classify that as teaching.

Such a description of directed, active learning fit observations of Corrine's
practice quite well. Students in her classes were often given information, which
was then followed by an activity designed to further familiarize students with
the content of the lesson. It became more plausible to Corrine that her students,
unlike herself, did not always learn science content by being passive receivers of
information. Corrine explained that the purpose of working with the information
was so students would have some time to "think through" the material. Though
Corrine displayed a sophisticated understanding of scientific inquiry, her ability
to make a distinction between the generation of scientific knowledge and the
personal acquisition of knowledge had only recently become clear. The role of
evidence in making knowledge claims linked the two ideas for her:

> Science is not a static thing. Whenever there's something we're looking
> at, they should be able to answer the question, "What is the evidence for
> that?" Trying to step them through explanations is more important than
> regurgitation, because if they don't understand why then it doesn't mean
> nearly as much. I'd rather have them apply the concept than just learn facts.

Initially, Corrine indicated in both the questionnaire and the interview that explaining or demonstrating science content accurately would be sufficient for correcting student misconceptions. Although she could hypothesize about student
difficulties with certain topics, Corrine did not really believe that students' prior
knowledge could influence science learning very much. When identified, student
misconceptions could simply be pointed out and corrected through explanation or
hands-on experiences.

During her practicum semester, a large part of her Methods of Teaching
Science course was devoted to examining student misconceptions and reading
research about the importance of student ideas and misconceptions in learning
science. Her ideas about misconceptions after this semester are best categorized

by the view that *student misconceptions are impediments to learning*. This was evident when I asked her how much she would help a student design an experiment to see if the principle of conservation of mass holds for plant growth:

> I would want her to go through most of it herself. . . . You have to be careful about designing this so it's not reinforcing the misconception, that they're getting their mass from the soil. . . . There's water to be considered. The whole idea is that it comes from out of the air, that plants are grabbing carbon dioxide out of the air and making mass out of that. So you don't want to reinforce the idea. I mean, evaporation could account for what she's seeing here, between water here and not here. So you want to make sure that she's controlled all those things so that she discovered it for herself. . . . I mean, the whole idea is to eliminate misconceptions, and I would not want to reinforce that. That would be a bigger problem for the student, to allow her experimentation to reinforce that misconception.

Corrine's answer to the same question a semester later was quite similar. Misconceptions mattered because they were barriers to learning, and were quite resistant to change. Corrine considered student learning through experience to be powerful, therefore she felt that teachers needed to ensure that they did not provide experiences that reinforced student misconceptions. As a result, she foresaw great potential for creating new misconceptions in the lab setting if procedures were not clear and direct.

Corrine also recognized that misconceptions could result from the way in which information is organized in the mind of the learner. She explained this idea using the example of her recent experience in a plant biology course, when her own conceptions about photosynthesis were brought to her attention. Corrine reported being struck by both the conception itself as well as the implications of having held it for so long, especially as someone with a PhD in a biology-related field:

> [The professor] outlined it on the board and I went, "Oh my goodness." The larger context of it clicked into place for me. . . . That *plant mass comes from the air*, really. I thought about it, I knew where everything came from. I knew plants made sugars . . . but the whole context of that, like what it really meant for that to be happening. I was stunned the whole day . . . a scientist for 20 years.
>
> I didn't study plants, so it's not something that I had been thinking about every day. But I've been a gardener, and it just never hit me in that way. So if it doesn't hit me as a scientist, how's it hitting Joe Schmoe on the street who doesn't have a science background, who doesn't think of things in that way? They don't get it, they don't understand the global context of it. I mean, I didn't! How many other people are walking around on the planet not getting it?

By the completion of her student teaching, Corrine had become much more aware of the various misconceptions students held about a number of topics, including photosynthesis and cellular respiration in plants. However, she continued to think of misconceptions as obstacles to understanding, and that eliminating them would be like unclogging a drainpipe to allow for the free flow of water. Leveraging student misconceptions as resources for student learning is a much more complex task, and is one that she will hopefully learn over time.

[]

During the last month of her student teaching, the Ridgefield School District began a period of organizational turbulence. The effects of personnel changes, budget issues, curriculum redesign, contract negotiations, and unexpected schedule shuffles for the science department all made a lasting impact on Corrine. Observing both school and departmental politics play out during this process impressed on her the importance of taking the larger organizational contexts into account when searching for a teaching job. She noted, "It's more than just the classrooms. There's a lot more that you have to consider, especially when finding a job. Just taking any old job could be setting yourself up for a miserable existence."

Corrine elected to spend a year at home taking care of her daughter after completing her program. She met with me again the following fall, with her preschooler in tow, and having read the case she affirmed its accuracy. As we talked, she once again emphasized the importance of finding a job in a place that had the right kind of professional community to support her as a new teacher.

"As a biology teacher," she told me, "I can be mildly selective about the position I take. I want to make sure I fit into the larger community." I felt comfortable enough with Corrine to needle her slightly about this outlook, and told her that some people deliberately took jobs in places that had very little in the way of professional community because that is where they felt they were needed most.

This brought forth a sigh, and Corrine told me, "That's not a battle I'm willing to pitch right now." She pointed at her daughter, who was playing with the toys in the corner of the coffee shop where we sat, and reminded me of the challenge of raising young children and starting a new career at the same time. Then she smiled, perhaps more to herself than to me, and added, "But maybe later."

CHAPTER 4

Creating a New Conception of Teaching

Armando—Biology, Chemistry

I don't think it's valuable to teach things kids don't want to learn. And if they don't want to learn something that's really valuable, then it's a failure on my part.

—Armando

As the 6th-grade students enter the room, Armando nods to Jethro, one of his fellow practicum students, who starts the video camera. Armando walks back and forth between the door and the front desk, greeting students and adjusting the focus on the overhead projector. The students are in various stages of situating themselves at their desks, but most take out notebooks and start copying from the screen. A few minutes later, Armando asks, "Who's not done? Raise your hand." Hands fly and Armando gives them an additional minute.

Ms. Cooper, the cooperating teacher, sits quietly behind her corner desk working on her computer. The classroom is large, but having 32 students seated face-forward at massive laboratory tables makes passage difficult for students and teachers alike. Armando reminds a group of off-task students that they should be copying down the data table on the screen. They have been making moon observations as a class, and the day's "do-now" consists of drawing the previous week's moon phase data from a projected transparency.

"Those of you who are done," he says, "clear your desks. We are going to be doing some pretty cool activities today. After a few slides." A student in the front turns to his neighbor and says, "This is why I love science. We always doin' something." Armando hurries the class to finish writing and shortly announces that he is waiting for quiet. One student in the front row shouts, "C'mon! Show him the respect you'd show your mama," and the class quiets rapidly. He turns off the overhead lamp and uncaps the data projector connected to his laptop.

The theme of the current unit is identifying patterns in data, and Armando's lesson plan for today closely follows the textbook section on scientific explanations. Satisfied that the students are ready, he asks, "Now, remember from last week, Mr. Tull was telling you about the Inuit moon legend?" One student calls out that the moon and sun were chasing each other. Armando nods and recounts the story from the science textbook briefly. "What were they trying to explain with this story?" he asks. A number of students shout, "Phases of the moon!" Some students become noticeably animated during this discussion, while others simply watch and listen. Armando leads a class discussion as he advances through his slides. His students continue to take notes from the screen.

Halfway through the period, Armando introduces the activity: "So, Mr. Tull and I were thinking about an idea that could be a scientific explanation to explain how the moon phases work. And we came up with this: I said 'I think the way the sun, the moon, and the Earth move around each other has something to do with the phases that we see.'"

A student from the back interrupts, "Do we have to copy this down?"

"You don't have to copy this down, just listen. So Mr. Tull said, 'I have a good test for it. Everyone knows that the Earth is a sphere, right?'" An affirmative chorus fills the room but one student calls out, "I thought it was a circle!" The students raucously seize on this statement while Armando waves his hand around the foam ball. "A circle is when you draw it on paper, but a sphere is when it's round like a basketball." He talks loudly over the students, "Okay, guys, I'm trying to explain the experiment that you're going to do for the next day. I'm not going to explain it any more times. I promise you I will not explain it again." The clamor subsides slowly.

"So, the way Mr. Tull and I would do this would be to take this sphere that looks like the Earth"—he holds up the foam ball again—"and let's just give it a sun. What kind of thing can be used to make an artificial sun?" Though many students are no longer paying attention, some in the front respond with "A yellow ball" and "Get some glitter."

Armando suggests using the overhead projector as a light source to represent the sun. He then begins to assign roles for the activity to students, who are seated in pairs at the lab desks; the person on the right will be the manager; the person on the left will be the communicator. The students' voices crescendo and Armando pauses thoughtfully. "Class," he says evenly, "I have a quiz. Do you want it right now?" Only half the class seems to have heard him, so he repeats his warning. He admonishes individual students and threatens the quiz a third time, adding, "And it is hard."

The class settles and Armando explains the activity in which the students are to model the Earth-moon-sun configuration during the lunar cycle. As they darken the room and students begin to move, one of the other practicum teachers alerts him that only a few minutes remain in the period. Recognizing that this is not enough time to do even the first part of the activity, Armando sends students back to their seats, opting instead to use the remaining time to return quiz papers from an earlier lesson. The students appear disappointed, and the noise level in the class rises again.

Armando attempts to quiet them calmly, but finally loses his patience and shouts at the class. Unlike the other three practicum teachers in his group, Armando rarely raises his voice, so this catches the attention of the students, who calm down and quickly take their seats. At the precise instant that order is established, the bell rings, and the whole fifth period science class rushes out the door to lunch.

🗍

Armando entered the Science and Math Teacher Education Preparation (SAMTEP) program at Briggstown University knowing that he would not seek a teaching job on completion of his certificate. In fact, he had no intention of ever becoming a teacher. He felt conflicted about sharing this information with the program coordinators, aware that many teachers leave the profession in the first years. Armando's concern was that his instructors might not put forth their full effort to prepare him for teaching if they knew of his plans, feeling that their efforts would be wasted on him.

The truth was that Armando had been offered admission to four different prestigious medical schools and his plan was to return eventually to his home country of the Dominican Republic as a successful doctor and open a school. "I already have my land to do so," he told me. "I want to build my own school, I want to do my own things. I just considered that to have a background in education is something that's crucial. It's not an aside, it's not something I want to ever leave." He saw enrolling in a teacher preparation program as a necessary step in the pursuit of this dream.

When a family member became ill just prior to the beginning of the spring semester, the financial strain placed on Armando's family was severe. The program coordinators worked to secure a teaching position for him within the city of Briggstown so that he could remain in the program and earn his certification through an alternate route, but their efforts proved fruitless. "I've been living on two hundred bucks a month," he told me after his first semester, "living off my savings for the last six or seven months. And it's been bad. I really don't want to stop doing this, but I really don't see any other option."

Ultimately, Armando was forced to set aside his plans to be certified as a biology and chemistry teacher, and he withdrew from the SAMTEP program, returning to his previous job waiting tables at a restaurant. By the following fall, however, his family's situation had improved and Armando was able to begin his program at the state's most prominent medical school. As a result of this withdrawal from the program, the 10-week practicum at Moshi Middle School was his sole field experience.

◻

Although the issue of preparing teachers for diverse classrooms has increased in visibility in the recent past, so too have critiques that these efforts often ignore the needs of preservice teachers of color (Cochran-Smith, 2000; Dilworth & Brown, 2008; Sleeter, 2001). Whether this occurs because teacher education programs serve an overwhelming number of White teachers with naïve ideas about student diversity or, less charitably, because teacher educators hold an implicit assumption that teachers of color already possesses the necessary skills, the fact remains that preservice teachers of color often have very different needs than do their White counterparts in learning to teach in diverse classrooms (Achinstein & Aguirre, 2008; Villegas & Davis, 2008).

As a university with a historic commitment to social justice and urban teaching, Briggstown was well positioned to leverage its resources to these ends. Yet in the weekly Methods of Teaching Science class meetings I observed over two semesters, scant attention was paid to issues of diversity. The year that Armando went through the program, the one-semester course that addressed issues of diversity and urban education was taught in the spring, after the SAMTEP students had already completed their urban middle-school placement and when nearly all were student teaching in suburban settings. I had a great deal of empathy for the program coordinators—their logistical challenges were complex, particularly in keeping the total time frame of the program to a single year—yet it remained the case that many of the Briggstown teachers were ill equipped to be successful teachers in an urban 6th-grade classroom after only a summer of coursework. As will be shown, Armando's needs as a teacher of color were sometimes different from the needs of his peers.

Not only had Armando been the only member of his science teacher cohort who did not identify as monolingual and White, he also had one of the group's strongest science backgrounds and continued to work part time in a neuroscience laboratory during the summer and fall semesters of his program. He was an active and engaged member of the methods classes I observed and did not share the disconcerting obsession with student discipline that some members of his cohort exhibited.

A cautious opposition to his peers was one defining feature of Armando's practicum experience, particularly with regard to the other members of his fifth-period teaching group: Jethro, Lily, and Jasmine.[1] Armando did not appear to seek out conflict and even seemed to go to great lengths trying to reach consensus on how the classroom should be run. Yet time after time, philosophical differences about learning, classroom management, the nature of the subject matter, and the abilities of the Moshi Middle School 6th-graders to learn science opened rifts that often left Armando standing against his three other team members. The Moshi Middle School demographics during the Briggstown University students' practicum—shown in Table 4.1—appeared to be a salient yet rarely acknowledged factor in the group's discussions.

Once during a class discussion in the science methods class, Armando tactfully suggested that the practices of his group were similar to those described in Haberman's (1991) article on the "Pedagogy of Poverty," which the cohort had read in a different class. Frankly, I agreed with Armando's assessment of his group. Haberman describes a list of systematic activities that often form the core of urban teaching to the exclusion of all else. His list includes:

- giving information
- asking questions
- giving directions
- making assignments
- monitoring seatwork
- reviewing assignments
- giving tests
- reviewing tests

- assigning homework
- reviewing homework
- settling disputes
- monitoring seatwork
- punishing noncompliance
- marking papers
- giving grades

Haberman makes a strong argument that this set of activities does little to foster learning, yet constitutes the bulk of what is considered "teaching" in urban classrooms. Armando, like Haberman, had concluded that the pedagogy of poverty did not work. Though it troubled him to do so, Armando eventually acquiesced to a number of these practices. His group members made no secret of their desire for Armando to be more of a team player, but in his view he had already compromised quite a bit. Disappointed with himself for going along with his practicum group, he later told me, "That's what everybody around me thought, and I kind of ran with it in terms of that situation. Again, it's a group. I'm the only person who thought differently, I wasn't going to achieve anything . . . I mean I tried."

And he did try. Prior to the entry of the Briggstown practicum students (15 preservice teachers spread across four periods of science classes), Ms. Cooper's students sat in groups of four at clusters of desks that had been pushed together for this purpose. After 3 weeks of teaching, the Briggstown practicum students voted (during their methods class) to turn all the desks forward so that students

Table 4.1. Enrollment and Race/Ethnicity Data for Armando's (and Jethro's and Kathy's) Practicum Teaching Placement at Moshi Middle School

Total Enrollment	American Indian	Asian	Black	Hispanic	White
793	0.4%	1.0%	88.4%	2.5%	7.7%

would be facing the front. Armando was the sole person voting against this move. The cooperating teacher also opposed the move because it made cooperative work more difficult, but she was willing to let the Briggstown students have control over this aspect of the classroom and learn from the experience. However, she did ask the Briggstown students to return the desks to the clustered arrangement shortly before the end of the practicum.

Armando also had a different perspective on the academic potential of the Moshi Middle School 6th-graders. As illustrated in the example of the sphere and circle explanation above, he saw the importance of having students make sense of concepts in their own "everyday language" before attempting to apply more sophisticated terminology, a practice supported by science education research (Brown & Spang, 2008; Warren, Ballenger, Ogonowski, Rosebery, & Hudicourt-Barnes, 2001). His expectations for student learning were high, but unlike the other practicum teachers in his group, he did not place great importance on the strategy of having students memorize information. Once when Armando and his group were designing a quiz, Jethro advocated for using only matching and true/false items. In this discussion he said, "Multiple choice tests are difficult for kids at this level." Armando, who was pressing the group to use more open-ended questions, responded forcefully, "I think you think these kids are handicapped!"

Perhaps the greatest tension within his group concerned issues of classroom management. Watching Armando interact one-on-one with students, I often felt as if I was watching a master teacher. His use of nonverbal cues with students was both frequent and effective. Where his classmates often raised their voices and became visibly frustrated, he was calm and generally unflappable. Armando regularly touched base with individual students and learned a lot about them in a short time. He listened to what they had to say and seemed to know how to talk with them in ways his group members could not. For example, once when Jethro was giving instructions to the class, a student in the back was tapping a pencil on his desk repeatedly, creating a distracting undercurrent to the lesson. Armando made eye contact with the student and the tapping stopped immediately. Later, when he began making the pencil noise again, Armando walked over to him, knelt next to the desk, and said quietly but firmly, "I am not playing about the tapping." That did the trick, and the student got to work.

Where Armando emphasized mutual respect in his interactions with students, his teammates routinely demanded compliance, which they were often able to secure through raised—often screaming—voices. Over time, the other preservice teachers resented Armando's unwillingness to be "strict" like them, portraying his choice not to do so as a weakness. His continued resistance to a points-based discipline system the others wished to implement (on the grounds that it simply didn't work) did little to smooth intergroup relations. Other factors added to this friction within the group. Armando's inclination to use texting instead of email as a form of communication became a particular sore point as the semester went on. His tendency to arrive late to class and planning meetings reflected a time-management issue that spilled over into his teaching.

Armando conceded that his one-on-one interactions with students did not transfer particularly well to the task of dealing with 32 energetic middle school children all at once, and he saw this as an aspect of his practice that needed the most work. Recognizing the importance of being able to productively address the class as a whole, he continued to struggle with ways to do it in practice. It took him somewhat by surprise that when he made a conscious attempt to improve his whole-class instruction, he found himself with the full support of his group. This was an issue they were all trying to address.

Given these experiences, it is worthwhile to ask if Armando even had the opportunity to change his conceptions about teaching. In fact, he did, for the reason that Armando had been actively and intentionally attempting to change some of his ideas about teaching science from the very beginning of the program. In the first weeks of his summer coursework, he told me, "I went to elementary, middle, and high school in the Dominican Republic. Teaching there was just the teacher standing up front, talking." As a high school student, he had enjoyed science, though he noticed that most of his classmates did not.

Armando told me that he saw the SAMTEP program as a chance to learn "a different way to teach science." In this way, Armando may have also been distinct from his peers. Findings suggest preservice teachers in the United States often draw on their own experiences as students as a resource to shape their teaching, sometimes even as a guide to best practice (Davis et al., 2006; Gomez, Walker, & Page, 2000; Hammerness et al., 2005). As will be shown, a number of Armando's ideas did change, and it is reasonable to ascribe some of these changes to the fact that he sought a new vision of science teaching to replace the unsatisfactory one he had experienced as a student.

☐

In our first interview, I presented Armando with the Census question, and he responded, "I would fall under Hispanic/Latino, but there are fifty-four Spanish-speaking countries. I normally circle in 'Other' and write in 'Dominican Republic.' I don't believe in race, I believe in ethnicity." He thought such questions had little value, and stated, "I always want to ask 'What information do you feel you've gathered when you ask this?'"

Our final interview took place on the day that Barack Obama became president of the United States, and we had both watched the inauguration in the Briggstown University student center shortly before sitting down to talk. When I showed him the question again he said, "I remember this, and I do still feel the same way, which is [that] it's a really meaningless question because I can't divorce myself from the fact I know and believe that there's no such thing as biological race." Armando felt that because there was such wide variation in the living conditions as well as the need to receive resources among individuals in a single group, the question itself had no utility. He continued, "Just as a quick example, Black. What is Black? I don't think a Black person from Louisiana [who] grew up in the deep south is the same as Barack Obama, who grew up in Hawai'i as the son of a White mother and a guy from Kenya. And Hispanic? There [are] fifty-two nations south of this border, all of them with their own cultures and fairly unique ways of viewing the world. So I think it's useless."

Armando maintained that directing resources at problems on the basis of race were misguided because "the divides that exist in America here have more to do with socioeconomics. . . . White kids in a poor area face the same challenges as everybody else, you know?" I pressed him further, asking if he felt that race played any role in society. "Biologically, race does not exist," he said. "Socially, it very much exists."

In discussing how the social existence of race impacts classroom teaching, Armando raised the issue of segregation. "Kids will always float to groups," he said, "but that isn't something to be unproblematically accepted by the teacher." Rather than point to specific issues of discrimination in the classroom, Armando saw a more generalized pedagogical problem of communication and perception. "I know teachers," he told me, "and I know they often fall into an attitude of 'Some kids are more capable than others,' or, just because they're so used to not getting a response from specific children, they gravitate just naturally towards those that allow the lesson to move on more."

Armando generally made charitable interpretations of the hypothetical situations I presented to him and aimed his criticisms at the pedagogical practices of the teachers, not at their underlying beliefs or social contexts, even when discrimination was clearly occurring. Yet in one scenario where a White student teacher singled out her African American students for discipline, he stated:

> It just seems to me that maybe she needs to be better aware of how she manages herself with children maybe she's not familiar treating. That's the reality of a lot of areas in the United States of America where people have little contact with people that haven't grown up in the same conditions they have.

Here, in acknowledging a link between life experiences and beliefs, Armando is also drawing a connection between a teacher's beliefs and pedagogy, but does not yet apply this idea to himself. Nowhere in the first interview does he broach the subject of how his own beliefs about students might influence his practice as a science teacher.

Entering the teacher education program, Armando had a somewhat canonical but open-ended view of scientific knowledge. "In science, we're not teaching assumptions, we're teaching what we can prove," he told me. His ideas about the pedagogical implications of student diversity were limited to the ways in which his students might relate to this content as presented in the textbook. For example, a textbook graph purporting to show "observed distribution of skin color" represented to him the results of well-researched scientific knowledge, in which he openly stated his confidence. When asked whether the racial or ethnic composition of his class would affect a discussion on the genetics of skin color, particularly as it related to this graph, Armando replied that it would not, "because the class is not representative of the general population, especially in the United States where neighborhoods can be segregated." Thus for Armando, the implications of teaching this topic to a diverse classroom of students were limited to whether or not the students themselves could be taken as an example of the content.

🗒

During his 8 months in the SAMTEP program, Armando's orientation to the nature of race, ethnicity, and culture appeared to change only slightly. He became less certain that the major problems with racism had been solved, but it became more plausible to him that race, culture, and ethnicity were irrelevant in the science classroom because he saw all students as capable of high academic achievement. His belief in the meritocratic ideals of schooling also seemed to strengthen.

In the final interview, Armando displayed a self-awareness about how his beliefs and actions as a teacher could influence classroom events that had not been present in our earlier conversations. In discussing various classroom scenarios, he offered interpretations such as "Maybe there's something I'm doing" and "Maybe I don't realize my true attitude." Similarly, he took responsibility for his students' learning in a forthright manner, saying, "If I can't interest them, I've failed."

Armando's views about the undesirability of segregation within a class did not change, but his thinking about the impact of lowered academic expectations developed significantly. He contrasted the lowered expectations held by his teaching group with another measure of his students' abilities:

I know those kids are much more capable of learning and retaining information, that they don't need a week of being presented the same—not even a higher-level—concept, but simple little things for them to memorize. No, I don't think that's right . . . you can ask any of those kids, tell me, sing for me the last—this is a silly example—sing for me the last rap T.I. put out. And they can spit out every verse, boom, boom, boom, boom. And each rap song has like four hundred, five hundred words, and they can memorize that stuff. You know? You're telling me they can't memorize the moon has five phases and how those five phases look?

In terms of the relationship between his students and the material, he maintained the importance of transmitting fundamental science information to his students, but developed a stronger desire to take into account his students' interests and the ways they interact with and relate to the material. He pointed to the "observed distribution of skin color" graph as he explained:

> I think it's important to go where the kids want to go. I don't know what's the more interesting part to them. Is it the fact that skin color is a polygenetic thing, you know? Is it the fact that skin color is even genetic and it's not something magical? Is it the fact that somebody-that's-darker-can-have-a-White-kid-if-they-have-enough-kids kind of thing? You know, so where they want to take it, that would probably affect where I go with my discussion of it.

I had not been aware of Armando's pursuit of an additional chemistry certification when we first talked at the start of his program. In January, I decided to present Armando with one of the chemistry scenario interview questions in the study, which asks, "Suppose you are studying sulfur bonds, and you use the example of keratin bonds in hair, and a student says, 'That's just in White people's hair right?' How do you respond?" Out of all the prospective chemistry teachers I interviewed, Armando was the only one to frame this question as an opportunity to use science to combat the negative self-image that non-White students might have about their hair. In this example, he describes how his response to such a question would depend on the racial and ethnic composition of his classes:

> A lot of images of self center around how you look. And hair is one of those things where people are like, oh you know, "Black people have bad hair, White people have good hair. Period. That's a thing in my country, White people have good hair, Black people have bad hair." And to be able to address that is something that very much has to do with the composition of my class. [To] be more specific, if my class were entirely White kids, I would probably have a small discussion, telling them the fact why other hair exists, so there's "White hair," and here's what Black people have—maybe go back to the theories of sub-Saharan Africa with the pestilence and the sun and stuff like that. And keep it maybe to that clinical level, maybe not explore any deeper. You know, for the sake of education. But if I had a diverse class I would probably set aside a whole day just to talk about that in different aspects, because it is something

that needs to be addressed. A lot of people aren't fortunate to have the figures in the environment of their life to be able to kind of deal with these questions and realize what society's throwing at them, and form their own perceptions, and hopefully come out with a positive image of themselves at the end.

By connecting the subject matter of the biology lesson to a goal that explicitly seeks to counter race-linked misconceptions, Armando is embracing a view of science education with a transformative agenda (Barton, 2003; Grant & Sleeter, 2003; Rodriguez, 1998). I remained uncertain of what role—if any—teacher education had played in developing this orientation, but clearly Armando saw a relationship between the content of science class and his students' well-being.

Despite his difficulties with group dynamics, Armando's greatest challenge appeared to be taking his deep knowledge of science and transforming it into lessons for his 6th-graders. Originally, he did not think it was plausible to teach science as a process to students before college, and felt that in order to make scientific knowledge accessible to high school and middle school students, it was necessary to oversimplify it almost to the point of being wrong. Especially vexing for him was pedagogy itself, though he clearly shifted during his time in the program from a strictly content-centered outlook on teaching to one where it was necessary to understand how students made sense of the content.

A number of aspects of Armando's view of science content as subject matter for students changed during his time in the SAMTEP program. First, his view of science as a large body of facts to be simplified for students gave way to a recognition that not all of the knowledge within a particular school science subject was of equal value, and that this realization had curricular implications.

Second, Armando was able to construct plans for teaching science processes to 6th-graders, refuting his earlier doubts. Though it was difficult to enact as planned, the lesson described in the opening of this chapter offers evidence of his effort in this area. Although he and his cohort relied heavily on the cooperating teacher for source materials, Armando was able to adapt these in a way that went beyond his prior notion that teaching occurs when teachers take difficult concepts and break them down into smaller parts. Watching his group members break down the content into smaller and smaller parts (e.g., devoting nearly a whole week to memorizing moon phase names) may have nudged him toward rethinking this view of lesson design.

His earlier conception of teaching also did not include much in the way of taking into account the students themselves, or the social context of the scientific knowledge. As noted earlier, this view changed significantly and Armando began

EDUCATION LIBRARY
UNIVERSITY OF KENTUCKY

to attend to the broader pedagogical issue of student motivation in his practice. When I asked what he would like to be able to do better as a teacher, he said:

> I think I would like to be able to follow along with where the class wants to go better. In the sense that, you know, you kind of have your goals set up at the beginning of class, you know, and you have your things the way you want to do it, and you prepare as much as you can, but the class might want you to go in a different direction in the sense that, things they're more interested about, or ways they're trying, thinking about the concept. [I would like to] be better prepared to react to that.

When I had asked him in the initial interview about what it meant to have a good understanding of science, he had spoken about how a good scientist can present concepts in multiple ways to multiple people. By the end of his practicum, he had developed a similar definition of good teaching:

> A good example is one of the people that we went to see during the Thursday nights when we went to visit teachers. He had a class prepared, he had a lesson. And of course he's been teaching for years, but he had six or seven ways he could teach that lesson. . . . And he said, "If a student said 'What if we did this and this and this and this?'" I'd say, "Okay, let's try that," you know. "But what if this and this and this happens? Oh okay." I could never say that. I'm like, "Well yeah, that'd be interesting, but let's move on with what I have prepared."

Armando's experiences in the schools of his home country had provided him with a conception of science teaching that he slowly replaced with a more student-centered vision that he perceived as more effective. Over time, he drew less on his own history as a science student and more on what he was learning in the SAM-TEP program about how to construct his vision of good science teaching.

Armando's conceptions about discipline and assessment underwent substantial changes, and seemed to be closely linked to one another. The example of threatening to give a quiz as a punishment for unwanted classroom behavior was actually a common occurrence that I observed in many student teachers' classrooms. Educators and education researchers have criticized such practices because they diminish the capacity for assessments to serve as an opportunity to provide students with feedback on their learning (Black & Wiliam, 1998; Glasser, 1990; Kohn, 1993). The prevailing conception among Armando's peers was that class discipline was necessary before any teaching could occur. How strongly Armando felt about this at the beginning is unknown, but a different conception—positing that good teaching was necessary before there would be class discipline—clearly became more plausible to him during his practicum. He felt that making students "accountable to the content" took priority over discipline, but this approach was difficult for him to implement.

From my perspective, Armando attempted to resist his groups' fixation on implementing ever-more complex classroom management structures while maintaining his own individualistic style, which he described as " . . . being laid back, [I] try not to escalate things." He recognized that each teacher had his or her own style of managing the class and that the Moshi 6th-graders took advantage of this. From this experience, Armando reported learning lessons about the importance of consistency and having students recognize a single classroom authority.

In reflecting on why most of his students had failed a quiz he had designed, Armando realized that he had made the test for his own pleasure and benefit rather than as a way to look for evidence of student learning. He described the moment when, under pressure from his group, he realized that what he was doing was a "totally separate reality" from what was going on in the classroom, and marked this realization as a pivotal moment in his process of learning to teach.

His group also had strong opinions on the appropriateness of the quiz, but it was difficult for Armando to untangle valid criticism of his assessment from what he perceived to be the unwarranted low expectations of his peers. In the interview, he explained how his group's low expectations had developed as a response to frustration with students, and emphasized that they were not overt or malicious. "Did we go in with a little bit of an unrealistic expectation? Yes. Did we overshoot it in the other direction? I think yes."

Over time, the pedagogical connections between task difficulty, student learning, and classroom management became clearer to Armando. He grew to reject his group's operating assumption that student misbehavior decreases when tasks are easy, noting that his practicum groups' simple tasks for their students were rarely followed by any noticeable improvements on tests. Armando and the rest of his practicum team interpreted this outcome very differently. During a discussion about this situation with his group in methods class, Armando claimed the students were bored by such a "dumbing down" approach and that it may have even been the source of some classroom disruptions. His group however, seemed to interpret the same poor test results as a reliable indicator of students' low academic ability.

There was one episode during Armando's practicum that has remained with me throughout the completion of this research, and I recount it here because it was an unexpected moment of importance—something for which educational research ought to always make room. I recall it whenever the topic of professional dispositions toward teaching students in urban schools arises, and remain somewhat skeptical that any sort of assessment can take the measure of a preservice teacher as well as this episode did.

Midway through the semester, Beth, another practicum student at Moshi Middle School, asked Armando to come into her class to help with an activity. Unaware of his career plans, she had asked him to pretend to be a doctor and answer questions for students during a unit on experimental design. A section of the textbook described a hypothetical flu treatment and had set the problem of evaluating a drug's efficacy based on different experimental designs, which Beth had turned into a realistic scenario.

The 6th-grade students had spent the previous two days analyzing the data sent in by "Dr. Sam" and had written to him with their results and prepared questions for his visit. Armando was introduced to class as "Dr. Sam," and he played the part—dressed in green hospital scrubs—without breaking character at all. "Hello," he told them. "My name is Sam Winatowski. I went to the University of Michigan for my medical degree and did my residency in Nebraska. I do emergency medicine by and large, so that's my background. I've been doing emergency medicine for about four or five years."

Armando's "Dr. Sam" led a class discussion, driven by the students' prepared questions about the drug trials. He described how he had bumped into the cooperating teacher and she had told him that she had a "very smart group of kids that was willing to do the tests." He also took time for other questions, such as where he worked and how long it takes to become a doctor. Unspoken but clearly evident throughout his interactions with students was his conscious presence as a role model. Watching the ease with which he made this transformation, it was impossible to avoid the conclusion that he was—for the moment—inhabiting his future self.

At his suggestion, Armando and I met in a downtown bistro shortly before he left for medical school. When he had finished reading a draft of his case, we ordered lunch and talked.

Characteristically modest, he told me that I had been "too nice," but agreed that the case accurately represented his thinking during his time in the SAMTEP program. He made minor corrections to the manuscript, but told me that the rest was okay to publish. He admitted some surprise at my favorable depiction of his teaching and classroom management ideas. Though his university supervisors had been supportive of him, he said that was the first time that his practice had been characterized to him in a positive light.

Armando expressed disappointment that he had not been able to finish the program but said that he did not regret a single moment. We talked a little more about SAMTEP, and then he started interviewing me about the town where I lived, where he would be moving for medical school. We finished our meal, and I gave him a ride back to his apartment. Since that time, I have followed Armando's progress in medical school from afar, and was recently amazed by a video clip of a research symposium in which he presented the results of cutting edge spleen research. I have little doubt that he will indeed fulfill his dream of returning to his country as a successful doctor and opening his own school.

Armando's case serves as a reminder that as powerful as the cohort model can be in teacher education (Darling-Hammond, 2006), care needs to be taken so that the needs of individuals—particularly teachers of color—can be taken into account in the design of these experiences. Armando was marginalized within his group, and not only did this serve to limit the ways in which his robust knowledge of students and class management skills could have benefitted them, it constrained his opportunities for developing his own talents as well.

Armando's story is also a reminder that preservice science teachers may have very different motivations for learning to teach science from the ones we might ascribe to them. Indeed, I have been surprised by the number of science student teachers I have known over the years who have not actually become teachers but have done something completely different with the skill set they have gained from learning to teach. Armando's story also makes me want to explore other ways for prospective teachers to inhabit their future selves.

CHAPTER 5

Searching for the Right Problems to Solve

Jethro—Physics

I've had to relearn and unthink some old ideas. In the physics realm I took some classes that were new, but I found my grasp of some of things that I supposedly knew wasn't all that good.

—Jethro

A student calls loudly, "Mr. Tull, you never gave us the labs back!" Jethro pauses and asks for the student to give him a couple minutes. He clicks on his laptop, and loud rock music begins to play in the classroom as the other physics students enter. Some students approach the front desk to ask about grades. Mr. Wilson, the cooperating teacher, sits in the back of the class grading papers.

A few more students approach the table but most linger near their desks. Some are working on today's "bell-ringer" projected on the front screen, which reads, "What do you believe happens when water changes from gas to liquid?" The class of 28 students is talkative and energetic. The period bell rings and the music slowly fades, leaving a silence in the room that does not last long. Jethro says, "All right, pass the bell-ringers up." Two months into his student teaching, this routine is well established. The students take their seats, but only a handful of note cards are passed forward; clearly not all are doing their bell-ringers.

Jethro holds the note cards and says, "All right. Everybody's concerned about grades; so let's talk about grades." He has their full attention and says, "The labs from yesterday are intended to be included in this grading period." He mentions that there were some misunderstandings in the previous day's lab, for which he feels responsible. "That's part of me learning to be a teacher," he explains before promising to clear things up today. He advances to a slide titled "Heat of Fusion Lab." Pointing to the fourth formula on the slide, Jethro states that the equation for percent error he had given them was incorrect because of the way he had written the formula. He talks through the equations for the next 10 minutes, and a few students ask clarifying questions, even though it is clear that many more are struggling. "Just crank through the numbers and get the answers," Jethro advises.

About 10 minutes later, after some slides about evaporation and condensation, Jethro asks his students to explain how a glass of water set out on a counter for several days might have no noticeable change in water level. He then walks behind his desk and points to a bowl of water that he says has been sitting out for a few days. "Why hasn't it evaporated?" he asks. There is no response from the students. Jethro then notes that the water is the same temperature as the room. He puts a thermometer in the water and announces that it reads 23 degrees.

One student is incredulous. He shouts, "It is *not* twenty-three degrees in here!"

"Celsius," Jethro says calmly.

"Oh," says the student.

Jethro waits a moment before presenting the answer on the following slide, namely, that the rates of evaporation and condensation are equal, and that the system has reached equilibrium. "We have condensation and evaporation occurring simultaneously," he tells the class.

He advances to the next slide and begins to discuss boiling. One student waves his hand wildly, and Jethro calls on him. The student asks, "If you have a hundred percent pure water, where do the little bubbles come from?"

"Mike's question is a good one," Jethro says, and his response is to explain that steam forms wherever the heat is. Another student adds, "It's like it's evaporating at the bottom." Jethro follows this with an attempt to draw a distinction between evaporation and boiling. He does so, however, without addressing the presence of dissolved gases or the actual phase transition from a liquid to a gas, stating simply, "All these bubbles are energy escaping the water."

Jethro keeps the class moving. He posts a slide asking "Why don't the bubbles form until the liquid reaches the boiling point?" A number of students raise their hands to offer their own ideas, but during these explanations he has the body language of a radio talk show host waiting for a rambling caller to finish. He is not wholly uninterested in their ideas he later tells me, but airing them in class this way tests his patience because it takes valuable time away from the rest of the day's agenda.

The next slide reads "What happens to the boiling point when the pressure is reduced?" Without much fanfare, Jethro walks behind the table and puts a beaker of water on a vacuum pump platform. He then places a thermometer in the beaker and positions a bell jar over the top, sealing it tightly on the platform. A video camera is pointed at the apparatus and a close-up of the beaker is projected on the screen.

In a very short amount of time, the water in the beaker begins to boil. In the absence of a heat source, the students are clearly perplexed. One student is vocal in his confusion. "So it's getting hot?" he asks. Jethro reads the temperature again and it is unchanged. He does not attempt to conceal his enjoyment—boiling water in a vacuum at room temperature is a classic physics demonstration—and there is pleasure to be had in watching students attempt to understand what is going on inside the bell jar.

After all of the students have seen the demonstration, Jethro turns off the pump and opens the valve to let air back into the bell jar. The thermometer on the video monitor indicates a sudden decrease in the temperature of the water. Taking notice, Jethro indicates that this temperature drop confirms what he has been saying about energy escaping.

One perplexed student, still looking at the beaker that had been full of "boiling" water just moments ago, asks, "What is the technical definition of 'boil,' then?"

Jethro's response is tentative. "I guess it means that you're applying enough pressure in order for the water to escape. . . ."

The next 10 minutes are consumed by another bell jar demonstration that simply does not work. Jethro places a small amount of water on top of an upside-down Styrofoam cup on the platform, secures the bell jar on top, and turns on the pump. Students sit and wait for something to happen, but the only visible action on top of the cup is the fizzling of little bubbles, making the water look like a soft drink. "All those bubbles are energy escaping from the water," Jethro tells the class. Mr. Wilson notices that the demonstration is not working and comes up front to help, but it appears there is simply too much water on the upside-down cup.

"I'm beginning to think this isn't going to work," Jethro eventually says with resignation. "What's supposed to happen," he finally tells the class, "is the water is supposed to freeze." Mr. Wilson asks one student to feel the temperature of the water on the cup, who reports to the class that it is very cold. Six more students come up front to dip their fingers in the chilly water.

The class ends with a surge of students to the front of the room, all asking about uncertain grades. As the next period's students enter, some of them join the swelling crowd at the teacher's desk to compete for Jethro's attention.

Jethro, a self-identified White male in his early 50s, came to the SAMTEP program at Briggstown University after retiring from a career in the information technology industry. It was a homecoming of sorts, because he had grown up in the area and had graduated from Briggstown University in the 1970s with one of the school's first degrees in computer science, as well as another in electrical engineering. Jethro's first job after graduation had taken him to a metropolitan area in the southeastern United States, which I refer to here as Mountain County, where he lived and worked for the next 30 years. He had his first taste of teaching when he was required to conduct technical workshops for his job, and involvement in organizing and coaching a youth bowling league had led him to consider teaching as a second career.

Relocating to the upper Midwestern United States from Mountain County held a number of challenges for Jethro, many of which influenced his experiences in the teacher education program. First and foremost, leaving the corporate world and enrolling as a full-time student necessitated substantial changes in both his personal and professional life. These were clearly challenges he welcomed as part of the switch to teaching, and he chose to pursue teacher certification in both physics and computer science. He arrived in Briggstown a year prior to entering the SAMTEP program and enrolled at the university as a special student to fulfill the science content course requirements for certification. He embraced being a college student again, and even lived in the university dormitories with under-graduates. His second challenge concerned the fact that the city had changed since his youth, and as the most senior member of the science teacher cohort, he continued to profess feeling both a geographic and generational disconnectedness even after his second year back in Briggstown. Finally, Jethro suffered from a num-ber of health issues that, though not directly attributable to moving north, were certainly exacerbated by the time he spent in Briggstown's aging school buildings. His classroom for student teaching seemed particularly problematic in this regard.

Jethro possessed a good-natured and infectiously optimistic personal de-meanor, and he was described by one of his instructors as "a smart guy, looking for the fun side of things, yet he's still serious. I think he's one of those [student teachers] who's going to have a good time with this because life's a playground, and science especially is a playground for him." Jethro often commented that what he learned from teacher education was of great value, and he seemed to draw on the approaches and methods advocated by professors more frequently than others in his cohort did, though he sometimes did so uncritically. He was diligent with his coursework, genuinely inquisitive about a broad range of topics, and meticu-lously organized.

Like the other Briggstown University students, Jethro participated in a daily practicum experience at Moshi Middle School for 10 weeks during the fall of 2008. In this experience, he had been part of a group with three other SAMTEP students—Armando, Lily, and Jasmine—assigned to a 6th-grade science class. As noted in the previous chapter, Jethro's practicum class contained little racial diver-sity; all but one of the students were African American.

Jethro's start in the classroom that October had been particularly rough, and he used words such as "nightmare" and "meltdown" to describe his first experi-ences in front of the 6th graders. His university supervisor corroborated this view, as did my own observations. Jethro and his supervisor both explained the issue as one of classroom control, exacerbated by Jethro's tendency to speak louder and become visibly angry when students were talkative or off-task. The significance of classroom management issues to Jethro's experience in middle school cannot be overstated. Most of his spoken communication and actions during his practicum teaching focused on securing individual and class compliance as a precursor to instruction.

Jethro collaborated closely with his teammates in planning lessons, yet he reported feeling constrained by the curriculum as well as by the cooperating teacher's insistence on sticking to established procedures, particularly when he had his own ideas about improving lessons. Over the course of the practicum semester, Jethro adopted a number of management strategies and suggestions from his university instructors and team members and, although he quite visibly grew more confident after his initial stumbles, he remained somewhat rigid in his expectations concerning student engagement with the subject matter. On the one hand, he was very accepting of the fact that students needed to talk with one another about the content. On the other, he frequently sought the attention of the whole class before continuing to transmit the content. These contradictory messages often led to conflict with students, which usually escalated out of control.

The following spring, Jethro was placed in a physics classroom at Briggstown Language Academy, a public magnet school specializing in world languages and housing middle as well as high school students. Jethro was assigned four physics classes, for which he assumed responsibility at the start of the semester in January. His cooperating teacher, Mr. Wilson, retained a single 9th-grade physical science class to ensure Jethro's workload was not overwhelming. In a city rife with residential segregation, Briggstown Language Academy was unquestionably one of the most racially and economically diverse high schools in the district, as shown in Table 5.1. Additionally, it was considered an academically successful school, with average state test scores regularly among the highest in the city.

Mr. Wilson shared Jethro's passion for physics and for dramatic demonstrations in particular. Although Jethro was able to draw from Mr. Wilson's repertoire of resources, activities, and labs, there was minimal communication between them about Jethro's teaching. Jethro regularly showed his lessons to Mr. Wilson before teaching them, but this practice was more about gaining approval than receiving feedback.

This lack of guidance and support was clear to me in my observations of Jethro's teaching, as if being a cooperating teacher simply meant handing over the reins of the classroom to someone else. After student teaching was complete, Jethro did not mince words. "I got more assistance and encouragement from the substitute teachers than I got from him," he told me.

◻

One of the most direct consequences of returning to college for Jethro was that despite his engineering background, the experience of taking science courses was largely one of learning new content. He noted that the field of genetics had advanced tremendously in the 30 years since he had taken college-level biology,

Table 5.1. Enrollment and Race/Ethnicity Data for Jethro's Student Teaching Placement at Briggstown Language Academy

Total Enrollment	American Indian	Asian	Black	Hispanic	White
1,083	0.3%	6.8%	51.9%	10.3%	30.7%

and in physics and chemistry courses he found himself with a new appreciation for the underlying mathematics in "relearning" topics he thought he had previously mastered.

An overarching conception for Jethro was that *teaching is primarily the act of conveying subject matter to students*, and this idea did not appear to change substantively over the course of his program. Given this conception of teaching, and struggling with the content as he did, Jethro remained wary about the prospect that a student might ask him a basic science question he would be unable to answer.

Throughout his time in the SAMTEP program, Jethro expressed the strong belief that a thorough and flexible knowledge of mathematics was required to learn physics at the high school level. His understanding of physics as a discipline was firmly rooted in his experiences as an electrical engineer and, more recently, as a returning student taking upper-level physics courses. Jethro initially felt that a mathematical approach to teaching physics was both the most genuine and efficient strategy. He was open to using a more conceptual approach, though he believed that doing so would require hands-on activities and take up valuable time.

The question of how much mathematics is needed to understand certain topics in physics has been debated in the field of physics education for decades. A robust program of conceptual physics emerged during the 1970s and 1980s and remains strong today, championed by physics educator Paul Hewitt through his *Conceptual Physics* textbook and supporting materials (Hewitt, 1992), a later edition of which was the text for Jethro's physics classes.

Jethro's conception regarding what it took to make "real" physics into conceptual physics was a process of what he repeatedly referred to as "dumbing down," a perspective echoed by his cooperating teacher. From the perspective of Hewitt and the conceptual physics community however, conceptual understandings are portrayed as foundational to understanding physics, a view well-supported by research (Hestenes, Wells, & Swackhamer, 1992). Hewitt also emphasizes the role of equations in a conceptual approach as guides for understanding the underlying physics and has argued that equations ought not to be used solely for the purpose of solving numerical problems (Hewitt, 2011).

Jethro had expected the mathematics in the course to be unproblematic for students because it was not calculus-based, and he assumed that students would be well prepared to work with equations and variables. When his students encountered difficulties in basic algebra and in solving simple word problems, his lessons often took much longer than expected:

My original idea was that the math at an algebra level was within the capability of all the kids in the class. As we moved on and I spent literally a week when we were doing waves, having the kids look at word problems and pick out what was frequency, what was period, what was wavelength, and solving simple formulas, they couldn't do it. Well, when I got to the waves we simplified it even more. And the kids [were] just not capable of reading two sentences and picking out the key terms and what they mean. And I couldn't bridge that gap, so I knew that doing mathematics in the class, from that point on, it just wasn't going to happen.

As the end of the year approached, Jethro was frustrated by the fact that he was not able to cover topics in sufficient depth simply due to time constraints. It had been the mathematics, not the hands-on activities, that had challenged him the most. Jethro interpreted his students' mathematical difficulties as a form of curricular friction, slowing everything down. His belief that mathematics ought to be a gatekeeper into physics strengthened, and his ideas about the nature of his discipline had ultimately led him to conclude that *students' knowledge of mathematics is the limiting factor that determines which physics topics can be taught*. Rather than recast his understanding of physics to accommodate multiple pathways for learning, he expressed a preference for students weak in mathematics to be "scared away" from taking the course.

I wish to be fair to Jethro here, and indicate that he regularly took responsibility for teaching students the mathematics they did not know and sought support from other math teachers in the school to learn how to do this. He often employed the time-consuming strategy of breaking down problems into smaller and smaller chunks until the individual pieces were manageable. From my perspective, it was somewhat like transmitting a novel by Morse code; Jethro's students were rarely painted the big picture or given an opportunity to develop conceptual understandings.

To Jethro, learning physics consisted primarily of following a well-worn path to understanding that led through advanced mathematics. This rigidity in knowledge of his own subject matter made it difficult for him to consider the alternate pathways to understanding physics that his students might travel.

In our conversations over the 13 months I followed him in the SAMTEP program, Jethro rarely referred to race, ethnicity, or culture unless explicitly asked. More commonly, when discussing the salience of diversity in the classroom, he would use the word "heritage," and occasionally the word "background," as proxy labels for race, ethnicity, and culture. He expressed a desire for demographic questions, such as those on applications or the census, to give him an opportunity to claim his eastern European heritage. He would, however, always answer "White" because, "as far as heritage, you know what they're getting at." He recognized that the major problems associated with racism had not been solved, but often used language that tended to downplay the salience of race in a given situation (Pollock, 2004). In fact, he seemed hesitant to assign race itself any importance at all, often seeking other variables besides race to explain disparate treatment or bias in situations both hypothetical and real.

His comments about his 30-year residence in Mountain County are instructive on this point. Mountain County was one of the places Jaspin (2007) profiled to document the expulsion of the Black population that had occurred there in 1912, and tracked the reverberating consequences of this "racial cleansing" event into the present. Despite its relative proximity to a metropolitan area in the southern United States with a majority of African Americans in its population, Mountain County has been and remains today predominantly White. In the 1980s, Mountain County attracted national attention when two White supremacist groups clashed with civil rights demonstrators in a series of protests that eventually led to a First Amendment case in the U.S. Supreme Court. Jethro compared living in Mountain County during this time to growing up in Briggstown during the late 1960s, when racial tensions over segregated housing policies escalated and the National Guard was mobilized in an attempt to avert the urban unrest flaring across the nation:

> The community that I lived in, when I moved there, there was not an African American in the community at all. None. I lived in [Mountain] County; it made the news and it was ugly. Very ugly. The African Americans would bus themselves into the county and hold demonstrations and so on, and this was like the KKK headquarters in the state. If you wanted to go into town just to sit on the sidelines for the excitement, power to you. But that was ugly. It was just like when I grew up here in the sixties. I didn't know enough about it when I was in the sixties, and in the eighties I was a mature adult I didn't think much of what was going on: why should people be treated like that? I thought, man, just no way.

This passage, as well as others from our conversations, offer evidence that Jethro associated race with notions of conflict and that he made a distinction between race and the concept of heritage, which he perceived as more benign. In reading this account, Jethro confirmed that this had indeed been his perspective. More will be said below about Jethro's observational—as opposed to participatory—stance toward issues of social inequality.

Jethro voiced optimism that segregation was less of an issue in Briggstown than it had been in Mountain County, though he admitted this view might have had something to do with his proximity to the university's neighborhood. In fact, shortly before he relocated from the south, Briggstown had been named in one study as the most residentially segregated metropolitan area in the nation (Iceland, Weinberg, Steinmetz, & United States Bureau of the Census, 2002).

The idea of contemporary discrimination operating systemically on such a large scale seemed implausible to him. Consequently, Jethro viewed residential and regional segregation patterns as either the result of self-selection or randomness. This outlook seemed to hold for all of his conceptions about why certain demographic patterns existed both in and beyond schools.

Like many preservice teachers, Jethro expressed a preference for seeing all students as individuals and resisted categorizing students by racial or ethnic group membership (Paine, 1990), though he occasionally did so. For example, during our initial interview Jethro said, "From the student groups I've worked with, I don't see many minority students who are interested in science, interested in math, and taking the advanced classes that get them into the college placement programs." Describing the characteristics of a particular group was not problematic for Jethro, as long as the description was based on his own experiences. Consequently, his ideas about the nature of racism led him to ascribe minority student placement in math and science courses to the motivations of individual students rather than to institutional or systemic explanations (Gamoran, 1992; Oakes, 2005).

Jethro's conceptions about the pedagogical implications of diversity were situated firmly in the task of ensuring student engagement. Responding to an interview question in which I asked how he might approach a group of nonparticipating Native American students in the back of his classroom, Jethro spoke earnestly about getting all students involved in learning. "If a student is in class and you can't find some way to engage them and you just think of them as 'That's the way they are, let them be,' they can't learn." When pressed further about what he would do specifically for this particular group of students, he reaffirmed his inclination to deal first with students individually, and then said that he would likely tailor the curriculum to meet their needs by "doing something special" for them. Other than including some historical content that related to the group somehow, he was uncertain what this "something special" might look like.

Jethro also felt that issues of diversity had little to do with teaching physics. When I first posed the hypothetical Van de Graaff generator scenario to him, Jethro erupted with laughter. He was admittedly unprepared for such a question and viewed it as a bizarre student misconception. Jethro stated, "Hair is hair," though he admitted that it was possible that hair products or styles could conceivably influence the effect of electrostatic charges on hair. "Why would my hair be any different from anybody else's hair?" he said. "I'd have to do a few questions and explore why they have a feeling [that] race has anything to do with hair and conducting electricity." Though this statement could be interpreted in multiple ways, it appeared to me that he exhibited an unwillingness to consider the possibility of race as a potential factor in this demonstration. For Jethro, at least in this early point of his teacher education program, race was about the past, implied a potential for conflict, and had little salience in physics.

⌷

One other conception about teaching that continued to surface during my conversations with Jethro over the course of the year was that *student engagement is necessary if teaching and learning are to occur.* Yet his conception of what constituted student engagement in a lesson changed over the course of his two field experiences. Although engagement remained for Jethro an effect achieved by external efforts at motivation by the teacher, he shifted from viewing *engagement as enticement to learn* to a more expanded notion of *engagement as ongoing attention to the content of the lesson.*

During his practicum and continuing into his first month of student teaching, Jethro's opening activity usually involved having students answer a trivia question. His conception of engagement required students to be connected somehow to the class and the teacher so that learning could occur. Therefore, Jethro did not perceive a need for his "bell-ringers" to relate to the content—they only had to be something fun or interesting to catch his students' attention. This was a strategy advocated and modeled weekly by Jethro's instructor at the start of each science methods class.

In the second month of student teaching, Jethro began to regularly use questions that directly related to the topic of the day's lesson. This represented a broader strategy for getting his students connected to the science content and not just to him personally. The openers were still designed to grab student attention, though now they had become part of a daily routine intended to get students thinking about physics. Jethro and I speculated together on what had brought about this change, and he pointed back to the group planning sessions during the Moshi Middle School experience as the source of this idea.

Jethro's use of music to start each class was representative of his original view of engagement as enticement to learn, but two additional pedagogical rationales emerged for this practice that had not been evident earlier. To Jethro, the end of a song represented the moment of transition from the hallway to the classroom, and he would begin his lesson shortly afterward. Additionally, he felt that the opening music offered an opportunity to build relationships with his students; in his youth Jethro had worked as a DJ, and he was up front about the fact that playing music for others was a way of sharing his authentic self with his students. He often accepted their suggestions for songs, and this gave him a chance to have conversations with his students about something other than physics.

In his final interview, he stated directly, "You can spout off facts and just because you're doing your job doesn't mean any learning is occurring . . . you do have to engage the students. If there is no engagement, then you're really not teaching." Over his year in the SAMTEP program, engagement had shifted to become not just a precursor to teaching, but part of teaching itself.

📋

Though Jethro had been trained as an engineer, he had little experience with scientific practice and the ways in which scientific knowledge is generated. Throughout his practicum and student teaching, Jethro described "the scientific method" and approaches to inquiry generally as a process of conducting experiments and thinking logically. Yet his notion of what constituted an experiment was largely atheoretical. Jethro was not the only one in his cohort who seemed to possess such a "folk theory" of scientific inquiry (Windschitl, 2004; Windschitl & Thompson, 2006), and he often seemed to conflate the terms *experiment, demonstration,* and *activity.* Throughout this study, Jethro's organizing conception about generating knowledge was that *inquiry is doing something to see what happens.* In his practicum lesson on the scientific method, he concluded the lesson by stating, "This is how real life experiments go. We set them up with a little bit of knowledge and we see how it goes."

To Jethro, inquiry represented a process for finding things out, but in practice his efforts to enact inquiry often remained unconnected to the learning goals of the lesson or to big ideas in the discipline. Being active in a science classroom was an end in itself, and Jethro considered his students' arrival at the "correct" conclusions in these activities as a form of positive reinforcement that would keep his students engaged and motivated in science.

This view of inquiry can be contrasted with one put forward by recent science education reports and reform documents, which stress a role for scientific inquiry as part of model construction and theory refinement rather than just hands-on activity (National Research Council, 2007, 2012). Duschl and Grandy (2008) describe this as a paradigmatic shift in the role of the laboratory in science education, depicting it as a change from "a view of science that emphasizes observation and experimentation, to a view that stresses theory and model building and revision," (p. 7). Jethro's opportunities to learn to teach in this way were constrained by his teacher education program's presentation of inquiry, which emphasized activities and learning through exploration.

Initially, Jethro expressed a preference for hands-on activities because he felt they better engaged students. Even when science activities were presented as fun, Jethro believed they also had to be experienced in the proper way. As a result, he felt it necessary to provide detailed instructions to students for each activity.

His orientation to student inquiry as a directed activity changed as a direct result of his methods of teaching science classes, which emphasized the use of a five-stage learning cycle model (Bybee, 1997) that encouraged teachers to let their students have some experience with phenomena before engaging in direct study. This approach was promoted by the SAMTEP program as a flexible way to think about lesson planning; it was not considered a rigid template.

Moving into student teaching, the notion of *student inquiry as exploration* seemed to guide many of Jethro's choices concerning hands-on activities. In the middle school, this practice had fueled Jethro's classroom management difficulties, but he attempted exploration activities again in his high school setting because of the high regard he placed on what he had learned in his SAMTEP methods courses. Eventually Jethro came to the realization that though exploration was still desirable in the learning process, it was a luxury requiring both time and resources. He returned to providing written directions for activities, but also tried to leave space for students to "play" with the phenomena. One example of this student inquiry as bounded exploration was the circuit lab Jethro did during the electricity unit. Though students were permitted to play around with the wires, batteries, and bulbs, the tasks he set for them were clearly defined.

Interestingly, and perhaps not accidentally, the conception that *inquiry is doing something to see what happens* also described Jethro's approach to improving his practice as a teacher. His preference for addressing classroom problems was to tinker a bit and "try something new" rather than to reexamine personal theories and assumptions about his practice. A number of his responses to hypothetical teaching scenarios, including "doing something special" for particular groups of students, were consistent with such a definition of inquiry.

One obvious example of his approach to inquiry in his own practice occurred when his physics demonstrations failed to work as planned—a common occurrence. Jethro saw these moments as an opportunity for students to engage in problem solving; he would solicit students' help in trying to figure out what went wrong. His approach to inquiry in these situations was generally consistent with a conception of inquiry as a process of trying something new to see what works. Rarely did he approach these situations systematically or attempt to solve problems by appealing to theoretical knowledge.

Overall, there was little evidence for change in Jethro's organizing conceptions about student diversity or its pedagogical implications throughout his teacher education program. Yet there exists some evidence for the emergence of new conceptions about the pedagogical implications of student diversity that were not evident earlier.

Although Jethro's conceptions of race and ethnicity existed under his umbrella of "heritage," the idea of culture and its implications for the classroom, proved to be more challenging for him to understand. Jethro told me that culture seemed to represent "the true part of a stereotype." In the following example, Jethro deployed culture as a concept to explain the behavior of his Hmong students in class, but then retreated to the more familiar idea of heritage:

> I think that as a rule, kids now are much more social than kids in the past were, and boys and girls talk equally as much. I don't think that's something that's differentiated by sexes. Might be by race, possibly. Might be by culture. I've got a few Hmong in my class, and they rarely speak out in class, they rarely talk in class. So if I had, for instance, a classroom full of a particular culture, it might be more so or not so more so, but that would have to do with the heritage more than anything else.

Though he rarely used the word "culture" in our conversations, he often did so in his course assignments. The semester he was student teaching at Briggstown Academy, he was also taking an evening SAMTEP course called Change Strategies in Urban Education—commonly referred to by students and faculty in the SAMTEP program as "the diversity class." The course was taught by an adjunct who was also an administrator in the Briggstown public school system. One of the primary texts for the course was Ruby Payne's (2005) *A Framework for Understanding Poverty,* a work that remains popular in teacher professional development circles despite increasing criticism that Payne's "culture of poverty" construct glosses over social inequalities and reinforces stereotypes about the poor (Gorski, 2006; Sato & Lensmire, 2009).

Jethro indicated that he felt that learning the cultures of his students was important, but what this meant exactly remained uncertain to him. He spoke of culture as though it were an inherent characteristic of a person and found it plausible that drawing on these characteristics to inform one's teaching would be a productive strategy, though he admitted being at a loss on how to do it. For example, in this reading response to a chapter in Payne's book, Jethro struggled with the pedagogical implications of having identified a particular cultural characteristic:

> *Understanding Poverty* suggests using checklists, having students write the steps out and [use] procedural self-talk as possible solutions. None of these seem to work with my students. I understand that there is little procedural memory used in poverty, but nothing I've tried seems to instill the necessity of completing step X before moving on to step Y.

For Jethro, the previously puzzling concept of culture had come to hold promise as a resource for maintaining student engagement, a task still central to his practice. Interestingly, Jethro did not yet invoke "culture" to explain student failure within school structures, an argument commonly voiced by prospective teachers

(Haberman, 2007; Ladson-Billings, 2006). For the time being, his explanations for student achievement remained primarily individualistic, but the conception that *culture is the true part of a stereotype* may prove too tempting as a ready-made idea for explaining student failure in the future, especially among students he identifies as culturally different from himself.

⬚

From the start, Jethro expressed a desire to form positive relationships with his students. His previous work with youth in the bowling league led him to think about some aspects of teaching as coaching. This was particularly true when it came to his attempts to motivate students to learn, and he often employed a cajoling style in his teaching, using phrases like, "C'mon, you can do this!"

Relating to his students proved to be a surprisingly difficult challenge for Jethro, for reasons that included generational, geographical, and cultural factors, along with all of the other personal, interpersonal, and social variables that influence human relationship-building. Despite repeated attempts, his efforts to form positive relationships with students bore limited fruit, and he felt this keenly throughout his middle and high school experiences. It actually came as a surprise to Jethro at the completion of student teaching that students wished to sign his yearbook, and he took this as evidence that perhaps he had formed better relationships with students then he had assumed.

Jethro's initial conception that *youth culture is relatively uniform* seemed to exert a strong influence over his approach to building relationships with students. It came as a surprise to me that during practicum, Jethro appeared not to make developmental distinctions between middle school, high school, and undergraduate students. Being on a university campus for a year had helped him to become familiar with the interests of contemporary college students, and he had simply extended this understanding of youth culture to his middle school students. He regularly chose examples and analogies that would have been more appropriate for undergraduate college students than for adolescents. Though not disagreeing with this notion when I presented it to him, Jethro maintained that it was more a matter of geography than age or culture:

> They talk about events that are happening locally here—I don't have a clue. Even things that I was familiar with in the city thirty-five years ago, they aren't here anymore. So they talk about nightlife, and things like that—I don't have a clue what they're talking about anymore.

From a pedagogical perspective, Jethro also saw the increasing value of tapping into student interests as a way to get students engaged in science. The trouble for Jethro was identifying those interests in the first place. During one of his middle school lessons, Jethro used the example of a video game he had seen his college roommate playing to discuss "the scientific method." The students were confused by his instructions to figure out the goal of a game most had clearly had never played. Using a supposedly "relevant" example such as a video game ultimately didn't work, and this was genuinely puzzling for Jethro. Rather than probing the interests of his students to develop appropriate examples, Jethro drew on his own impressions of his students' interests and sense of what was relevant. To put it mildly, these impressions were not always accurate.

As he moved from the middle school to the high school, working with a different age group provided Jethro with some solid experiences on which to base his decisions of relevance. He also became more aware that some of his teaching practices were not well suited to his students. For example, he noted, "I've been teaching adults so long that my humor with students isn't always appropriate." He appreciated, in a way he previously had not, that his efforts to form positive relationships with students were hindered by the fact that aside from music and sports, he often didn't know what his students were talking about. This, he recognized, made it difficult to tap into their interests.

His conception concerning the uniformity of youth culture was eventually replaced by the idea that *youth culture is differentiated by what is appropriate for different age levels, particularly within schools*. Although such an idea may appear obvious from the perspective of basic developmental psychology, to Jethro this realization represented a significant insight into student behavior. Notably, it was also a perspective that did not invoke the concepts of race, ethnicity, or broader notions of culture, which held little explanatory power for him anyway.

⬚

In both his practicum and student teaching placements, it appeared as if student diversity held little relevance for Jethro. In talking about what he learned as a result of his middle school experience, he ascribed his difficulties primarily as they related to students' age levels, and the challenge of teaching 6th-graders. Drawing on students' culture for curriculum or pedagogy, or as a resource for understanding and solving classroom problems, was something he had not been prepared to do.

During the second interview, between his practicum and student teaching, Jethro had laughed again at the Van de Graaff scenario, and was even more emphatic about the irrelevance of students' race and ethnicity in the physics demonstration:

> I remember I had the same reaction! Why? Why would you think it would perform differently on anybody's hair except possibly if there was some

coating on the hair? So my question would have to be, "What would lead you to believe there's a difference?"

I prodded him further, and asked how he would respond if the student said, "C'mon Mr. Tull! White people's hair and Black people's hair are different, right?" He responded:

And I would say, from a biological standpoint, I don't believe they are. The color may be a little different, they may be a little thicker, they may be a little thinner. But they have the same types of materials in them, and again, I go back to the same thing: If you use a hair product on your hair, that may make a difference, but that's got nothing to do with race.

What is interesting about this is that Jethro appears to have greater confidence in his knowledge of physiology than his teaching or his personal history would support. He indicated that he had taken his first university biology course only the previous year and, in the initial interview, his discussion of this experience offers a glimpse of his view of the discipline:

I found that in several cases, the stuff that I was getting was new. It didn't exist thirty-five years ago, when I was doing this stuff in high school and college. Biology has changed so much. The biggest example I can give you is in genetics. What was there to really teach when I was a high school student? There wasn't that much knowledge. There wasn't even that much knowledge about the cell.

Jethro's insistence that the irrelevance of race to this demonstration seems driven not by his knowledge of the underlying science but by his desire that it should not matter.

Nonetheless, he recognized that such a question about the role of race in the Van de Graaff physics demonstration might provide an opportunity to study something of interest to the students while simultaneously addressing perceived administrative requirements:

It might be an opportunity to investigate a little bit and learn a little bit more about the heritages in the classroom. What kind of conceptions do the kids in the classroom have about some of the heritages that might be available? We could spend some time exploring some of that. Give me an opportunity to do that multicultural thing, as far as the classroom goes. I'd have to make a sidetrack on it, but that doesn't bother me any. If we have an opportunity to learn a little bit more about backgrounds, our heritage, why not? I don't see why I couldn't waste a day and do that. You know, it's a goal somewhere in one of the standards, so gee, I get to knock that one off, check that one off the list somewhere.

Although he did not necessarily view such an opportunity as relevant to physics or having inherent value, he did view it as a way to motivate students and encourage their participation in the class. He could also "do that multicultural thing," which to him represented an externally required imposition on his classroom time. When asked what concerns he might have in taking this approach, he stated, "I just have to make sure that we stay focused and there's no slurs that are thrown around the classroom." This notion of student diversity as primarily a source of conflict was still evident in his student teaching at Briggstown Language Academy. He observed self-segregation among students when they got to choose their own groups, and noted, "There are individuals that cross [racial boundaries in groups], and those are things you have to watch in class."

In his Change Strategies in Urban Education class, Jethro was assigned an article (Key, 2003) that explored the multicultural education concepts of *content integration* and *equity pedagogy* in the context of teaching science to African American students.[1] In a written reaction to the piece, Jethro stated that the idea of integrating multicultural content into science made little sense to him. Though he perceived value in, as he put it, "rewriting science topics statements to include scientists with specific heritages," he concluded:

> In my opinion this is not practical. I can and do include heritages with long histories in science achievement. In physics, very little time is spent dealing with modern physics and it's usually left as the last unit to be covered, in case there is little time left. There are a few scientists of African American and Hispanic heritage in modern physics and these can be highlighted. This means teaching content out of order.... As I completed this reading I couldn't help but think how impractical this is in the field that I teach.

The concept of adapting his pedagogy for students of different demographic categories was even more difficult for him to grasp. He wrote that he wished more examples had been provided in the reading, other than "using sports-related vignettes to teach physical science," and ultimately protested, "We're left to invent these things for ourselves." Even the sports example is puzzling to him because, though it seems potentially relevant to students, it simply does not connect to Jethro's notion of "heritage" in any specific way. To Jethro, *multicultural education means exploring heritage in a school context*, a definition that for him leaves little room for physics. Yet for the first time, there is evidence that he is aware of another way of viewing multicultural education, even if he is not quite certain what it entails.

When we talked in June, Jethro described his school's diversity as "a real positive thing," and saw this diversity benefiting himself as a teacher. He noted, "My class was so diverse, I got to experience a little bit of everything." These benefits of diversity apparently extended to the students themselves, as was evident when Jethro used his cooperating teacher's Van de Graaff generator during a lesson on electrostatics. Appreciating the irony, he reported that the question he had found so funny in the previous two interviews had actually been posed to him by a student during this demonstration:

> "Will it affect my hair differently than your hair?" was the way it came up. I said, "Well let's look and see how it affects my hair first. So you guys can see. So you're going to come up and volunteer, right? Yeah, no problem, okay we can do that. Now we need some other comparisons. Well, our hair is both short. Mine is gray yours is not. What's the difference? I use nothing on my hair, you probably use something else." Well, I had plenty of girls with long hair, so I could go with that. But I had—this class was so mixed, I had Hmong in the class, I had Spanish heritage, I have African American heritage. I had a lot to choose from. But all the boys predominantly had short hair. . . . I had one boy with medium-length hair, and fortunately, he volunteered.

Although this conversation held no discomfort for Jethro, as it might have for others, the question of the role of race as a factor in the demonstration was quickly subsumed into a long list of other potential influences. Yet, for the first time, he was aware of race and ethnicity affecting his teaching in the present, not in the past, as his conception of heritage would have demanded. Furthermore, even though the salience of race and ethnicity was downplayed, it was not denied, and remained for Jethro a variable connected unambiguously to the physics content of his lesson.

After sending Jethro a draft of his case, we met in the basement eatery of the Briggstown University student center. Over pizza and drinks, he told me, "It was difficult to read some of those things about myself, but once I thought about it and decided it was the truth, I kept reading."

He told me that he had completed his physics certification program and planned to continue earning his master's degree, but reported that the school had not lived up to its end of the bargain by providing him coursework and fieldwork in earning his other teacher certification in computer science teaching. His frustrations with the university bureaucracy had been a frequent topic of our conversations throughout the year. Finally Jethro set legal action into motion against the university, and very quickly he was offered a computer science student teaching assignment for the coming fall semester. Though this meant delaying his job search, Jethro accepted the student teaching assignment. At this writing he is teaching high school physics, chemistry, and physical science in the Briggstown Public School system.

Jethro's case serves as a reminder of some of the challenges faced by second-career science teachers. For him, these challenges included learning new science content and forging relationships with students in the absence of a shared generational culture. Being an older adult in a physically stressful job within a school environment had also put strains on his health, impacting his opportunities to learn to teach in his student teaching placement.

However, one of the most striking aspects of Jethro's case concerns the way in which he framed his own organizing conceptions about teaching and students. Although teacher educators and policymakers attend to factors with clearly defined "achievement gaps" such as race, ethnicity, and class, Jethro focused more on the geographical and generational distinctions he perceived between himself and his students. He all but dismissed efforts to draw attention to issues of race in his teacher education program because he simply didn't see a connection between physics and his conception of diversity as historical heritage.

Although students in the Briggstown SAMTEP program were often prompted to examine their ideas about science pedagogy in their methods classes, Jethro's own ideas about diversity were not elicited and held up to examination in the same manner. Had this occurred, his instructors might have been better able to reframe his notions of heritage into more powerful analytic lenses that would have allowed him to learn more as a teacher.

In particular, his view of the problem of geographical and generational differences between him and his students offered an entry point for Jethro to "study the students," an important aspect of effective teaching (Darling-Hammond, 2006). Developing a deeper understanding of his students' communication styles, as well as the ways they thought about and used mathematics in their lives, would likely have been of great benefit to Jethro. Yet, without these explicit connections in his teacher education program, Jethro was, as he put it, "left to invent these things" for himself.

CHAPTER 6

Discerning the Role of Student Experiences in Learning

Kathy—Biology

> After a while I just get claustrophobic inside. That's the hardest part about being in a classroom every day.
>
> —Kathy

As her seniors enter the environmental science room, Kathy sits calmly at the computer in the corner behind the demonstration table, entering grades and attendance into the school's database system. She is staring closely at the screen with her back to the door but, as the room fills with the sounds of adolescent conversations, she turns and waves hello to her students. There is a calm and unhurried atmosphere here, as if this class has somehow escaped the relentless modern pressure of standardized testing and school reform.

Mr. Garner, the cooperating teacher, emerges from the prep room and chats with the incoming crowd. Though the room is windowless, it feels like a place to learn about nature, and it is not hard to imagine that we are really in a cabin classroom in the woods. Every available patch of wall is covered with taxidermied mammals, nature posters, bones of all kinds, and environmental bumper stickers with varying levels of political overtones.

Students take their places at the four long rows of black lab tables in the front of the room, and Mr. Garner disappears into the back as the bell rings. Kathy makes a few final keystrokes and then walks to the door to greet the trickle of late-arriving students. The classroom banter is loud, and Kathy tries to get them settled. "All right guys," she says as she walks to the front desk, "we've got to get going. We're going to the park today." The seniors take their time, well aware that graduation is less than a month away. Kathy calls students by name in an effort to quiet them down. "Jeffrey. Ryan. Julie." Eventually she has the attention of most of the class.

Kathy points to the front whiteboard, which reads "Canoe slips due tomorrow! $25 trip, $10 t-shirt (optional)." "I need your permission slips," she says. "But make sure you turn it in all at once. The sooner you get it in, the more likely it is we'll be able to guarantee you'll be with your friends." Students are evidently excited about this trip, and it takes Kathy a minute to settle them again.

She lifts a magnetic compass from a box on the front table and holds it up to the class. "Remember, today you're just taking down information. We'll make the map tomorrow in class, and your grade will depend on how close the end point on your map is to the actual end point." The students begin to rise from their seats, but Kathy isn't finished. "You all know the way there. The only thing I'm asking is that we all cross at the lights and we cross together."

Going outside is a familiar and welcome routine for the students, and the class walks down to the corner of 88th Street and crosses together. It is one of the first truly warm spring days of the year, and though Chambersburg High School is in a densely populated and busy area of the city, it feels like a nature hike. Students are relaxed and talkative; some form shifting interest groups on the sidewalk while others walk alone in quiet contemplation. As we pass a front yard with pink and white magnolia trees in bloom, one student plucks a flower and proceeds to pull off the petals absent-mindedly. I hear the word "prom" float through the air more than once.

Six blocks later we regroup at the edge of the park near a large grassy triangle formed by the intersection of three walkways. Though Mr. Garner is present, this is clearly Kathy's class, and she takes charge. "This is the triangle that you're trying to get to," she says. After a quick head count, she leads the class through the park to a large pavilion alongside a landscaped pond.

At the pavilion, Kathy outlines the main points of the orienteering activity, which is part of the unit on land use developed by Mr. Garner. "Look at the sample on your worksheet and find the triangle I just showed you." The students are attentive as she holds up the worksheet and points to their current location. "You can go any way around the pond," she says, straining her voice to be heard by all. She then holds up a compass. "Just remember to point your arrow, Fred, until red is in the shed." It takes me a moment to realize that she is calling the compass arrow "Fred" and is not talking to a particular student. I later learn she has adopted this memory aid for using the compass from her cooperating teacher. The students nod and start forming groups. "Remember!" she calls, "I don't want to see just two people in a group doing all the work. If you have a third person, have them count off paces also."

The groups begin their task, and a number of them work so quickly that they are soon far away from the pavilion. Kathy works patiently with two students who are having trouble reading the compass, but they are soon on their way.

Students travel around each side of the lake, and Mr. Garner walks with some on the far side while Kathy walks with a smaller group on the other. Three students decide to go over a hill instead of around it, and Kathy catches up to them to ask if that will affect their map. "It wouldn't matter," the pace-counting student answers confidently. "The up cancels the down."

"We'll see," says Kathy.

The compass activity takes a total of 12 minutes to complete, and now that all of the students are accounted for, the return trek to school begins. Somehow it does not take as long as it did on the way there. One student says that she is sorry she wore heels.

Once back in the classroom, Kathy collects the compasses and announces, "You made good time. So you have a few extra minutes." High school seniors know a good bargain when they hear one, and most sit in their seats and talk for the next 9 minutes. Kathy takes the opportunity to chase down a few students for missing assignments, hand out some last-minute permission slips, and chat with students in the front row. Her seniors carry their conversations out into the hall after the bell rings, but many wave goodbye to Kathy, who stands at the front desk waving back and watching them go.

With a degree in natural resource management, Kathy spent her first 4 years after college working as an environmental educator in various nature centers across the United States. Her last job had been with an urban ecology center in the city of Briggstown, and the experience of designing, planning, and teaching lessons in partnership with city schools had left her feeling much like a science teacher already. The rewards of getting to know particular groups of students over the course of a school year had convinced her that she would enjoy teaching. The idea of finishing a certification program in a single year appealed to her, and she began her summer courses in the SAMTEP program at Briggstown with enthusiasm.

Describing herself as an outdoors person, Kathy expected that being inside all day would be only one of her personal challenges in becoming a teacher. "I need to work on being a force in the classroom," she told me early in her program. "I'm naturally kind of quiet and shy, so it takes a lot of effort to be animated." She also knew that being a biology teacher required venturing beyond her expertise in environmental science. Learning about genetics well enough to teach the subject was a recurring concern of hers in our conversations over the year.

Though eager to begin her 12-week practicum experience, Kathy approached the prospect of working closely with her three SAMTEP peers with apprehension. She told me that in her prior work experience, collaborating with colleagues had usually been challenging and unproductive. Her group's practicum assignment was a 6th-grade science class at Moshi Middle School in which all of the students were African American. As the semester progressed, she expressed relief that her practicum group had similar orientations toward grading, planning, and classroom management. They used a rotating schedule for assigning lead teacher, and usually two of them would run the lesson while the other two observed the class. "This didn't prevent the students from trying to play us off one another," she told me.

During the second week of teaching, one of Kathy's group members brought a large-display digital timer into the classroom, an older model of the kind commonly seen in racing events. Whenever the 6th graders began to get off-task or become inattentive, one of the group members would start the timer and let it run until the students quieted. The total time that accumulated on the display during the lesson became the length of time that students were then held after class. The timer was simple to operate, and other SAMTEP practicum students in earlier periods also began to use it as a favored classroom management tool. Doing so fit the conventional wisdom of the cohort, namely that student behavior was primarily a matter of external control by the teacher.

Kathy resisted using the timer, though occasionally one of the other practicum students would start it for her if the class was disruptive. Though not completely unflappable, Kathy's approach to classroom management was noticeably different from that of her group. Whereas the other practicum students often became visibly angry and yelled at students (intolerably, in my view), Kathy rarely did. Though she often felt the same frustrations as her colleagues did, she simply didn't view yelling as productive. "I'm not a screamer and I don't like it," she told me during her practicum semester.

Eventually Kathy's practicum group agreed to use clapping signals to get students' attention, a strategy she employed much more often than raising her voice. To Kathy and her practicum colleagues, order and quiet were the necessary initial conditions needed for learning. The group's agreed-upon strategy for achieving these behavioral goals was by using rewards and sanctions. Kathy was comfortable with her group's attempt at positive reinforcement, but as with the timer, she had her doubts about using punishment as a teaching tool.

From her experience at the nature center, Kathy knew that children often "act differently outdoors," and she regularly lobbied to bring the 6th-graders outside for a lesson. She was consistently overruled by her group, however, who told her that the students "couldn't handle it."

Kathy's full-time student teaching placement was in an environmental science class at Chambersburg High School, located in the working-class suburb of Briggstown where she lived. In the mornings, she also spent time with a different teacher in a 10th-grade general biology classroom, planning and leading lessons on some days and observing on others. Kathy had greater responsibilities in the environmental science course and soon became the lead teacher for three classes each day.

Mr. Garner had been an environmental science teacher for 19 years, the last 12 of them in Chambersburg. His classroom had been a reliable placement for many Briggstown University student teachers in the past, a valuable asset in the complicated process of identifying and selecting cooperating teachers for secondary science placements each year. Consistent with his philosophy of how people learn to teach, Mr. Garner intentionally spent most of the time at his desk in the back prep room while Kathy was teaching so that she could "feel like she has her own class." He had high praise for Kathy right from the start, and wrote on her mid-semester evaluation: "Working with Kathy is like working with a veteran teacher rather than a student teacher." One unfortunate consequence of Mr. Garner's confidence in Kathy was that she rarely received feedback from him on her teaching because he did not watch her lessons with any regularity.

Kathy's seniors had a variety of motivations for being in the environmental science course. Though many students clearly had a strong interest in the subject, the class also had a well-earned positive reputation for its many field trips, a factor that both Kathy and Mr. Garner said kept enrollment high enough to justify five sections of the course every year. Although Kathy generally followed Mr. Garner's curriculum for the course, its elective nature meant that there was plenty of room for her to try out her own ideas.

In my initial meeting with Mr. Garner, he mentioned that there had been a significant shift in the makeup of the school population since he had started teaching there. "Things are changing here," he told me as he described the district's recent demographic trends. Chambersburg High School had indeed been changing. According to state documents, 93% of the students a decade earlier had identified as White, compared with 68% at the time Kathy was student teaching, as shown in Table 6.1. Kathy recognized that her 10th-grade biology classes represented this demographic profile far better than the elective 12th-grade environmental science classes, which were nearly all White.

At the time of this study, the state's open enrollment law had been in effect for 10 years, and its primary purpose was to allow students to enroll in schools across district boundaries. Mr. Garner, who was White, portrayed these changes as unwelcome. He expressed to me his belief that this law was the primary reason for the school's changing demographic profile and on occasion made comments to me about the way the school used to be, and I worried a little about what effect Mr. Garner's attitudes might have on Kathy over time.

Table 6.1. Enrollment and Race/Ethnicity Data for Kathy's Student Teaching Placement at Chambersburg High School

Total Enrollment	American Indian	Asian	Black	Hispanic	White
1,459	2.4%	2.6%	9.7%	17.1%	68.2%

The classroom management challenges of her middle school practicum were mostly absent from her student teaching, and her students were generally compliant with her classroom management efforts. Her teaching consisted primarily of a well-planned sequence of activities for her students, though she continued to struggle with maintaining an authentic connection between grades and student learning. Observing Kathy in her environmental science classes, I was often struck by how consistent her practice was with the vision of good teaching advocated by the instructors in the SAMTEP program at Briggstown.

📋

At the beginning of her program, Kathy expressed the belief that students ought to be treated as individuals and that she did not consider race to be important. Although she was quite willing to discuss race and racism, even raising the possible issue of prejudice by White teachers toward students of color, she did not necessarily accord the concept of race much power or relevance.

In our initial conversation, I presented her with a copy the U.S. Census question on race and ethnicity and asked what she thought about when she saw such questions. She answered, "I respond as White but I usually think that it's irrelevant to whatever form I'm filling out." She thought a bit before continuing, "But working with some of the jobs that I have, we do keep track of some of the ethnicity of our students because it helps us get funding—working with different minorities. But usually I find it irrelevant."

Kathy was not alone among study participants in dismissing race and ethnicity category questions as irrelevant, yet it was striking that she also recognized that funding for her work at the nature center depended on responses to them. The logical connection between funding and the participation of "different minorities" was vague for Kathy. She perceived this funding as an incentive or reward for keeping minority student participation high, and most of her SAMTEP peers—White and non-White alike—held similar beliefs.

The actual rationale for the collection of these data is quite different from what Kathy had in mind. Testifying before Congress about the design of racial categorizations for the 2010 U.S. Census, Sharon M. Lee described the historical and current reasons for the collection of race and ethnicity information in government documents, noting:

> Racial statistics had historically functioned to maintain a social order and policies that excluded non-White groups from civil and political rights. The civil rights era dramatically changed this, and racial statistics are now used to document racial discrimination, leading to new laws and policies to redress systemic racial inequalities. (U.S. Commission on Civil Rights, 2006, p. 4)

Rather than viewing the collection of race and ethnicity data as a way to ensure nondiscrimination in the application of state and federal funds, Kathy saw this effort as an attempt to control institutional behavior through rewards and sanctions. As a result, Kathy's conception of race itself remained largely unmoored from issues of institutional and systemic racism.

Mentioning it almost as an aside during our first conversation, Kathy said that she had maintained a mentoring relationship with an African American 6th-grade girl named Tashanna for the past year. Kathy often referred to Tashanna as her "little sister" because they had been paired up through the organization Big Brothers/Big Sisters. Tashanna came from a low-income urban background, and her comments on school and science offered contrasting perspective to the views Kathy brought from her own suburban, White, middle-class upbringing.

Kathy said that her mentoring relationship had forced her to think about issues of race because Tashanna would raise the topic in their conversations. "I used to tiptoe around race," Kathy told me, "but working with my little sister, it was in my face all the time and I had to deal with it." Although Kathy agreed that major problems associated with racism were not solved, she tended to speak as if these were isolated problems experienced by individuals, and thought that contemporary discrimination was mostly unintentional.

At the beginning of her program, Kathy told me that potential racism on the part of teachers might be influenced by the way the media portrays different ethnicities:

> It may not be intentional, but, I mean, everywhere you look it's White culture, and it just makes me think about my little sister and she says that her White teachers—she has a mix of White and non-White teachers—and those White teachers, she says, are racist and they put all of the non-White students in the back of the room. It gets me to thinking . . . it might not be intentional, but maybe there's just some deep-seated reasons for that, some underlying issues that need to be brought to teachers' attention.

Kathy's conception at that time was: *Racism requires malice, but discrimination does not.* Her orientation to racism as an individual rather than a systemic problem is also evident in her responses to Tashanna's reports of racist teachers in school:

> During Black History Month she said they weren't talking about it at all in her class, and that really bothered her. So I tell her that she really needs to step up and say something or go out of her way to learn something new about the topic she wants to learn in school—take responsibility for her own learning. I try to reassure her that that can't be the case; teachers are not out to get her or any other student.

This suggestion demonstrates how Kathy is trying to be supportive of both Tashanna and Tashanna's teacher. To Kathy, mindlessness, not racism, is a more realistic explanation of the teacher's behavior, and her idea of a proper response is for Tashanna to be both assertive and self-sufficient. The idea that structural racism is a system that permits unintentional discrimination to occur as common practice was not yet part of Kathy's thinking.

Untangling the social, developmental, and cultural influences on learning science was not a task that came easily to Kathy at the start of her program. She was disturbed by her little sister's negative attitude toward science, for which she blamed both Tashanna's "addiction to television" as well as her "coming from a broken home." She told me, "I don't see her parents pushing her to achieve in science."

Kathy viewed Tashanna's knowledge of science from a deficit perspective, focusing mostly on what her little sister did not know and could not do. She also felt that Tashanna was missing some basic experiences with nature, what journalist Richard Louv (2005) has termed "Nature-Deficit Disorder." Kathy also recounted Tashanna's complaint that "her teachers haven't made the subject interesting for her, and she doesn't feel motivated to do any of the projects they assign her." This was an area in which Kathy worked hard with her little sister, trying to share the wonder of science that she herself felt. She sought to provide her with fundamental experiences in nature, taking Tashanna for walks in the woods and going to the beach to look for shells.

Kathy agreed that race, culture, and ethnicity could be relevant in the biology classroom but said this related more to science content than to pedagogy. When I asked how she might respond to a student who wants to know if genes for skin color are related to other genes, she cited the linkage between people of different ethnicities and some genetic disorders. Admitting that she had not yet taken her required genetics course, she confessed to being unsure of the scientific details of this connection.

The notion that one's pedagogy might be influenced by student diversity seemed unrealistic to Kathy. In talking about a lesson on the heritability of skin color, I asked her how the racial or ethnic makeup of her class might influence the lesson. She considered this at length, and then said simply, "It wouldn't."

Over her year in the SAMTEP teacher education program, the most evident change in Kathy's thinking about diversity in the classroom related to making science relevant and engaging to her students. She began to view identity and culture as resources upon which she could draw to engage students in science, and recognized that cultural differences could influence communication between teachers and students and ultimately affect student learning. The idea that culture informs perceptions and shapes thinking had also become more intelligible to her, and this prodded her to reevaluate her past experiences with Tashanna. Yet Kathy rarely found it necessary to invoke the concept of race to explain discrimination, and without an understanding of the social dimensions of race to guide her thinking, Kathy found her students' talk and behavior about race puzzling. As will be shown, this left her uncertain as to how to respond to racist behavior in the classroom.

Kathy's initial perceptions about the link between student engagement and perceived relevance occurred in her practicum at Moshi Middle School, and later served to create a base on which to build her understanding of the pedagogical implications for student diversity. She described how one of her lessons was floundering until a student "rescued it" by making the topic relevant to the other 6th graders:

> It was about how a disease had spread through a community way back when in England, and the kids did not relate at all. And I noticed that there were no ties [in the textbook] to modern day, or where the kids were coming from. It was about vaccinations, and I don't know if it was smallpox, but the kids had no idea what was going on or couldn't even really relate to that time period. I think one kid—he was a repeat student so he had seen this the year before— he kind of spoke up and linked it to getting vaccinations today and having to go to the doctor and get shots. Then I think kids started to really catch on to what we were talking about.

Over the fall semester, Kathy showed an increasing awareness of "identity and culture" as aspects of her students' lives. She continued to think about these connections largely in terms of how culture could be made part of the content, and referred to how a required course on Native American history, culture, and tribal sovereignty helped her think about these curricular connections:

> Overall I walked away thinking that there's a lot of things, especially in the [Briggstown] area, that you could draw upon that might relate to Native American students, or any students really, especially when you're thinking about science and natural resources—there's a lot of things in the community that you could link your activities to.

A section from Kathy's final paper for her Change Strategies in Urban Education course demonstrated the extent to which Kathy had enriched her thinking about the pedagogical implications of student diversity over the year of the program. She wrote:

> While the majority of urban teachers are White and middle class, the majority of urban students are non-White students in poverty. Many teachers

live outside of urban centers, where it is generally considered taboo to discuss race and skin color.

She then described how teachers should acknowledge stereotypes but embrace cultural differences and search for students' strengths. Her paper concluded with specific implications for using these ideas for teaching:

> Teachers may then begin to understand the ways in which urban students learn and how culture can shape student perceptions. Teachers must also make a conscious effort to avoid lowering their standards and expectations of multicultural students. Instead, teachers should provide additional resources and build upon the prior knowledge and experiences that students bring to the classroom.

What comes through in this piece of writing is a sense of the importance of student identity and culture in student learning. Whereas earlier her ideas were limited to incorporating diversity content into biology lessons, in this work (written during full-time student teaching) she referred to building on the prior knowledge and experiences of "urban students" and embracing strengths and cultural differences. Equally apparent, both here and in other data, is the fact that she has little notion of how to apply this idea to her teaching. In particular, understanding "how culture can shape student perceptions" is singularly difficult for her because Kathy's own understanding is that culture is related to the outward expressions of beliefs, practices, and traditions, and is not something that affects perceptions. Though she spoke earlier of "culture," in the paper she raises the notion that the discussion of race and skin color is "taboo" in the suburbs, where she also notes many teachers of urban students live. Although she uses the language of culture ("taboo"), she does not refer to the culture itself. This, and her other use of language, such as the phrase "multicultural students" indicates a view of White culture as the norm to which other cultures refer, defined by the existence of the "Other" (Apple, 1993; Chubbuck, 2004).

Kathy portrayed culture as a resource for participation and engagement but did not yet view it as a lens through which lived experience was interpreted. This was evident in one of her practicum lessons on the phases of the moon, in which she used a textbook section on "moon legends" from different cultures. Kathy's understanding of the authors' rationale for including different cultures' explanations for the phases of the moon was to keep the interest level of the students high as they distinguished between testable and untestable hypotheses.

Ultimately, it was in teaching the topic of evolution in biology class the following semester that Kathy was able to comprehend more clearly how culture shapes perception and influences learning:

I noticed, especially when we started talking about evolution, there were a lot of strong opinions that students brought with them, and a lot of them were based on their religion or their culture. You know, when you've got students just blurting out that they don't believe you and that this is a bunch of baloney, it's hard to ignore. So I've started to think, I can't just assume that everybody's the same; they all come bringing their identity and their beliefs with them.

The idea that learning can be strongly influenced by beliefs made more sense to Kathy when she was able to connect it to the more familiar example of resistance to learning evolution. By the end of student teaching, this realization had led Kathy to recognize the necessity of learning more about her students in order to be effective as a teacher. Having just interviewed for a middle school science position in Briggstown, she considered the implications:

It makes me realize that I need to look beyond just the content I'm teaching, and I need to make it more relevant . . . I need to learn more about students, different minority groups, different ethnicities, and kind of predict what students are going to be bringing to the table, what their beliefs are going to be. And I'm looking at a school now where the population is one-hundred percent African American, and it's got me thinking. . . . How am I going to meet the needs of these students, knowing that I grew up a whole lot differently than some of these urban kids?

Earlier, Kathy's conception of culture had been represented by elements external to the individual, such as stories, behaviors, and practices. Now, by attending to student beliefs and the effects of those beliefs on learning, she has accorded her conception of culture some internal power as well. However, precisely how to take student identities and cultures into account when planning and implementing lessons remained a challenge for her. This issue of knowing what to do but not knowing how to do it—sometimes called the "problem of enactment" (Hammerness et al., 2005)—is of great concern to teachers and teacher educators alike.

Insight into this problem of enactment can be gleaned from Kathy's lesson plans because of the conspicuous nature of the disconnections between changes in her thinking and her actual practice in the classroom. I examined 41 lesson plans prepared by Kathy for her environmental science class for spring student teaching. These lessons covered a wide range of topics, including sustainable forestry, mining, wilderness survival, wildlife ecology, and animal tracking and trapping. Despite the relationship of many of these topics to the strong Native American cultures in the area and Kathy's stated intention to draw on such resources during our conversations prior to student teaching, there was no evidence that she used any of this material in her lessons. A similar examination of the 16 lessons Kathy prepared for her 10th-grade biology class, which mostly covered topics of molecular genetics and inheritance, revealed a similar absence of multicultural content. The idea that multicultural content was primarily for "multicultural students" held firm for Kathy throughout her education as a teacher.

After reading the above section in a draft of this chapter, Kathy herself offered a three-part explanation for not including culturally relevant material in her lessons. "First of all," she said, "it didn't occur to me. I didn't know to include that material. I took what I had in front of me, and in the stuff Mr. Garner gave me, it wasn't there." It seemed that in her biology and her environmental classes, the seemingly fixed nature of the curriculum made it difficult for her to incorporate multicultural content, even given her apparent freedom to modify her cooperating teachers' activities. The second reason was what she called "the time issue." Kathy found that modifying her cooperating teacher's lesson plans often required a significant investment of time, something that she had less of while taking her SAMTEP courses three nights each week. Finally, she noted she had not included content from the Native American Studies class because she was not teaching Native American students. "I don't know if I would have even considered it relevant to that group of [Chambersburg] students," she said. Kathy saw the integration of multicultural content into her lesson as appropriate primarily for students who might relate culturally to that content, even though it could have been of considerable value for all of Kathy's environmental students.

Once Kathy started viewing culture as consisting of more than an external expression of one's upbringing, she was able to re-examine some of her past difficulties with her little sister. During practicum, Kathy had remarked on the odd similarities between Tashanna and the Moshi Middle School students in a number of respects: "They're impulsive, they have a hard time keeping track of things, and their stories never agree!" She also noted how their stories seemed to be told in the same roundabout manner. At the time, Kathy began to situate such communication issues firmly within a developmental framework, seeing them as generalized characteristics of 6th-graders.

By the completion of student teaching, Kathy had come to label some communication issues as having cultural dimensions and was better able to disentangle them from issues concerning child development. Although she had previously considered Tashanna's habits of "talking in circles" and interrupting to be personal quirks, learning that storytelling, circular patterns of talking, and interactive dialogue could be cultural norms made her reassess these communication issues. She noted that this realization had made an immediate impact on the way she viewed her classes: "In biology, some of the students would interrupt while I was talking, but it'd be related to what I was saying. It wasn't because they were being disruptive, it was because they were trying to participate." Kathy suggested that these types of communication issues might be responsible for the differential academic achievement of White and non-White students, an idea she clearly had not held at the start of her program.

⌓

Though there was considerable activity in Kathy's thinking around issues of culture, she continued to feel that the concept of race had little explanatory power. If anything, her idea that *invoking race for explanations carries negative consequences* actually became stronger over her year of learning to teach. She saw mentioning race, even in the Census identity question, as having the potential to reinforce negative self-images. Although she thought that discussing the genetic basis for skin color was an appropriate activity for a biology class, Kathy expressed a preference for choosing different genetic traits, such as cleft chins or attached earlobes, to explore heredity. To her, using these examples left less room for students to make unwelcome comments about skin color:

> Students may use skin color as a put-down almost, as a way of making a student feel bad. So I may hesitate, just because of some of the comments I've heard. So maybe I might think that the students aren't mature enough to take it as data; they might use it as a personal attack.

Kathy's strategy for creating a safe classroom environment for her students of color entailed keeping a lid on such unpleasantness, even if it meant bypassing certain content.

During the year of this study, Kathy rarely used race labels, either in speaking with me or in her lesson materials. In her only student teaching lesson that referred to skin color, Kathy prepared an activity for her students that included the following set of instructions:

> Draw a human pedigree that shows a man and a woman with three kids. The oldest child is a girl, the middle child is a boy, and the youngest child is a girl. The youngest child is an albino. She marries a man with normal skin color, and they have a baby girl who is an albino like her mother. What are the genotypes in this human pedigree?

Human skin in this problem has been reduced to "normal skin color." Although Kathy is certainly limiting the language of this problem to make the simple Mendelian model of genetics understandable to her students, it is consistent with the conception that: *race has limited relevance in the classroom and need not be invoked for explanations.* As will be shown next, such a conception made it difficult for Kathy when invoking race eventually became necessary for explaining classroom events.

⊓

Kathy clearly brought a sense of moral obligation to her work. Her lessons on the environment often connected with issues of fairness, in terms both local and global. She was unfailingly kind and even-keeled in her classroom demeanor and appeared to form positive relationships with her students. Her good rapport was often extended to those who might be socially isolated or fall through educational cracks. She had made a sustained commitment to working with Tashanna and planned to make a career out of teaching students in urban public schools. In short, Kathy appeared to possess all of the necessary professional dispositions for teaching in diverse classrooms (Gollnick, 2008; Villegas, 2007).

Yet, as much as Kathy had learned during her teacher education program and from her little sister, the lived experiences of race remained a mystery to her. By the end of her program, she still saw racism as something individual and malicious. Though the idea of systemic or institutional racism may have been intelligible to her in an academic sense, it did not seem likely to her that such things could have the same pernicious effects as individual acts of discrimination. The result was that she found it incredibly difficult to accept what Tashanna and her students told her about their experiences with racism. This is clear in the earlier example when she reassured Tashanna that her teachers were not out to get her. She also found it difficult to believe her Moshi Middle School 6th-graders when they said that some of their teachers were racists.

For Kathy, even though the notion that *race is irrelevant in the classroom* became less plausible, it remained strongly held because she had nothing else to take its place in her conceptual ecology. That is, she was not able to think of a way in which race *could* be relevant. One possible answer comes from Tatum (2003), who notes "Black youth think of themselves in terms of race because that is how the rest of the world thinks of them" (p. 53). The fact that such an idea was not yet accessible to Kathy in her thinking became clear to me during the following incident in her classroom.

In Kathy's second month of student teaching, Paul, a White student in her afternoon environmental science class drew a racial caricature of an African American classmate on the electronic whiteboard. He had been acting as the class data recorder during an activity on population growth during the incident. Of the 26 seniors in the class, Devin was one of only three African American students. "Look!" Paul had shouted in the midst of the activity, "It's Devin!" Most students were involved in rolling handfuls of dice and did not notice the drawing. Neither did Kathy, who had been reprimanding a group of students in the back of the room for being off-task.

One student saw it, however, and shouted, "Draw the lips bigger!" The next round came quickly, and Paul and his helper deleted the caricature as they returned to their data-recording roles as each group called out their tally of population changes.

At the end of the period, while Kathy was organizing and putting away materials, Paul once again drew a caricature with a wide nose and big lips, this time with the whole class watching. "Devin, someone drew you!" shouted one student. Another student called out, "I don't think you drew the lips big enough." Paul continued to revise his drawing as his classmates laughed until the bell rang moments later. Devin left the class with a clear look of shock on his face.

Kathy and I had watched this scene—which lasted all of about 30 seconds—from opposite sides of the room. Later that evening, in an email to me, she wrote: "I immediately erased it from the board, but as students were rushing out of the room, I didn't know what to do. I was appalled, but given I wasn't feeling well and my head was a little fuzzy, I didn't think to get Devin's reaction. I had hoped he hadn't seen it."

I returned to observe the same period the next day, but no further mention was made of the incident by anyone. I encouraged Kathy to discuss what had happened with both Devin and her cooperating teacher, even if the result was only to acknowledge its occurrence.

During our final conversation we discussed this incident at length. To my surprise, the majority of her remarks concerned Devin's culpability, even though he was the one being portrayed in the racial caricature:

> I've seen Devin instigate more stuff than I've seen them, so I almost wonder if they followed his lead. I almost think that they would be much more sensitive of that and not even draw pictures like that or make comments like that if it weren't for him and the way he jokes about himself.

Kathy reported numerous other incidents of Devin "poking fun of himself" in front of his classmates, some of which she found offensive. Although Kathy came to understand many of the general behaviors of her high school seniors, particularly those concerning their social needs and desire for independence, she simply could not understand Devin's continued invocation of race in situations where it seemed unwarranted to her. She gave another example:

> We were going outside and there was a little window well with a grate over it, and Devin said, "That's where they keep all of the little Black children," or something like that. You know, just little random comments. He's just pointing: "Yup, that's where they keep them." And I looked at him and he just shrugged his shoulders, and you know, [it was] just some weird little joke, just some running joke for him.

Kathy's perplexed interpretation of this incident—and her subsequent depiction of Devin—suggested that she had yet to come to terms with the impact that racialized experiences have on the minds her students.

Kathy's hesitance to intervene in the caricature situation was rooted in the fact that she had not quite defined the problem. To her, the problem could have been one of instigation (in which Devin would take the blame) or classroom management (in which Paul would bear more responsibility). The problem might also simply be one of violating the "taboo to discuss race and skin color," as she had written earlier. The common denominator for all of these explanations is that the harmony in the class has been disrupted in some way, making things uncomfortable. Stating "I had hoped he hadn't seen it" was a further indicator of a desire to maintain good classroom relations rather than to view this incident as a teachable moment for Paul and the class.

Not yet comprehensible to Kathy was the possibility that this problem may be one of a classroom climate that supported and perpetuated racism. My own (admittedly anecdotal) impression shaped by observations of teacher-student interactions in the public spaces of the school was that the Chambersburg School environment itself seemed generally hostile to students of color, which may have contributed to this particular classroom's climate. When I suggested to Kathy that Devin's actions might have been a way to cope with such an environment, she pointed to his defensiveness whenever she questioned him: "There were times where he would just put in his headphones and just tell me to leave him alone."

Kathy never mentioned the other students in the room, White or Black, who witnessed or participated in the incident, and it is evident in this silence that this remains an individual, rather than a collective, issue for her. Though she might wish for a classroom environment free from racial conflict, she had not yet developed the skills to combat racism in the classroom. It is also likely that the possibility of addressing this issue beyond an individual basis would have created unwanted conflict with Mr. Garner. Indeed, Kathy's discussion with him about the incident was less than supportive. She reported his response to be "Oh, it's not a big deal. These kids just goof around."

The idea that *race is not significant in the classroom* would seem credible to Kathy if she accepted her cooperating teacher's explanation of the incident, but she did not. Kathy continued, "It bothered me because some of the stuff this student would say, this African American student, I found offensive. But here he's talking about himself and poking fun at himself. I have no idea what's going on with him." For the time being, the conception that *race is significant in the classroom* had become more plausible to her, but it did not yet have the power to help her understand Devin enough to empathize with his experiences.

Over the course of the year, Kathy's perspective on the role of student ideas changed significantly. Before beginning the program, she strongly agreed that clear explanations by teachers were able to correct student misconceptions. Though she was aware that students held certain misconceptions about particular science topics, she did not see how knowing about these would help her teach students any better. At the end of student teaching, Kathy described her initial ideas about student misconceptions this way: "I thought that if you tell students something, and they disagree, then they'll take your word for it and suddenly understand."

By the end of student teaching, Kathy had expanded her understanding of students' ideas in three particular ways. First, she was able to give examples of particular misconceptions students might possess about different topics without much difficulty. Second, she had come to see how the use of student ideas related to their motivation for learning. Third, she began to speak of student ideas as the raw material of learning rather than as interchangeable bits of information, as she wrote in this reflection:

> When the teacher uses a student's idea to generate discussion, it takes into account what the students are thinking. It's not just throwing information at the students, but taking their ideas, their preconceptions, and getting them to talk about it and maybe . . . instead of just telling them the answer, getting them to think about it and come to their own conclusions.

Kathy had revised her earlier belief that clear explanations were enough to correct student misconceptions. The tenaciousness with which learners hold on to their misconceptions had become apparent to her, both in her SAMTEP courses and in her fieldwork. She now felt that students learned best when they figured things out for themselves instead of being told or shown.

From the start, Kathy had expressed a desire to involve her students in learning that was "active" and "hands-on" and rely less on the use of lectures as a teaching strategy. Following her practicum, Kathy reiterated her commitment to providing her students with the opportunity for "hands-on learning." When I asked her to define what she meant by this, she said, "To me, I guess it means that the kids are doing something . . . it's them actively asking questions or making observations or really problem-solving versus just being lectured to or talked to."

At the mid-point of her program, Kathy simply desired to have an active classroom. Yet by the end of her student teaching, it seemed unrealistic to her that "hands-on" or "active learning" alone would foster student learning, preferable as it was to lecturing. A project to create solar cookers in the environmental science class—one of her cooperating teacher's signature lessons—did much to change her thinking about other elements that fostered science learning, particularly the idea of ownership over the curriculum. In describing the project, she told me:

> They don't have too many opportunities to really claim ownership for a project. We usually do these shorter labs, but with this four-and-a-half-day lab, it was really there, and you could sense the pride in these weird contraptions that they had made. It made me start to think that maybe I should try to incorporate a little bit more of that. . . . If I really want them to claim a project as their own, it really needs to be a problem that they're in charge of solving. I'm not there giving them the steps and telling them what to do in the process.

In a very short space of time, Kathy had come to see much value in the idea that *student ownership of work supports meaningful learning.* This led her to reconsider the meaning of the grades she assigned for such a project, a dilemma she was just beginning to confront. This new focus on the internal motivation of students to learn science, or at the very least to participate in the activities of the class, was significant.

One other aspect of Kathy's thinking that changed during this time was that she became less certain about indicators of student motivation. As mentioned, the environmental science class took numerous field trips throughout the semester. The cost of these trips was borne entirely by students, and any students who were unable to pay for the trip were not permitted to go. At the beginning of the semester, Kathy considered those who went on the trips to be the "motivated ones." Although she felt that her seniors were "nearly adults and responsible for their own learning," she reconsidered the economic dimensions of the field trips. When I asked how her thinking had changed over the semester, she replied:

> It has changed a bit, because at the beginning of the semester I was given the impression by my cooperating teacher that those who went on the trips were the motivated kids, and the kids who didn't were the slackers and they didn't bother to get their permission slip in. But towards the end, after I got to know the students and they would come to me and tell me their sad story, whether it be their car or whatever . . . I started to see that maybe it wasn't just because they weren't on top of things and maybe it wasn't just not being motivated to get the permission slip signed, maybe it was financial. The problem is that field trips are not really open to all students, because not every student can afford them.

In this statement, it is clear that Kathy was reconsidering not just the economics of field trips but the validity of her indicators of student motivation as well.

◻

Kathy and I met in a small suburban coffee shop on a crisp Sunday afternoon in November, 2 months into her new job as a 7th-grade teacher in the Briggstown School District. She had been hired on the day before classes began in September and was teaching in what she termed "a very diverse middle school." Admitting that it was strange to read about herself, she expressed her satisfaction that this write-up of her case "captured things pretty well." She added, "It showed where I was at the start, and at the end how I was still unsure of some things." Kathy described how reading the case brought back some issues that she hadn't thought about recently, particularly making content more relevant to students' lives. "I've just been caught up in teaching, and don't really feel like I have any time to step back and think about this stuff," she reported, adding that the lack of resources at her school make it "hard to put the teacher ed[ucation] tools into play."

She did not feel this inability to use what she had learned in SAMTEP represented a shortcoming of her teacher preparation, however, noting, "My main focus some days is not on teaching. It's discipline. Sometimes I feel like a warden." She reported being surprised by other teachers' attitudes. "I got to the school," she said, "and almost immediately I ran into the attitude that inner-city kids are hopeless. I wasn't prepared for that reaction."

In so many ways, Kathy remains primed for tremendous growth as an educator, and she possessed at the start many of the personal and professional qualities needed by master science teachers for diverse classrooms. What this case shows is that she responded and grew along those dimensions in which she had an opportunity to learn (e.g., fostering student ownership over learning), and that her progress was stalled in areas that were not a focus of her program (e.g., addressing issues of discrimination). It may be that Kathy's considerable motivation to make connections with her students will help her find allies to resist the negative attitudes she currently encounters. Though the actively moral dimension of Kathy's social consciousness remained untapped by her teacher preparation program, my hope is that it may yet give her the strength to push back against those who would try to socialize her otherwise.

CHAPTER 7

Permitting the Implications of Diversity to Emerge

Roberta—Chemistry

> My sophomore year of high school, I walked into my first chemistry
> class and everything simply clicked—the years of bathroom-laboratory
> experimentation, speculation about what the world was made of, and a
> general aptitude for science finally made sense. This is what I was meant
> to do, chemistry was my calling.
>
> —Roberta

It is a morning in late April, and Roberta lingers by the classroom door greeting her 8th-graders as they enter and settle in their desks. Closing the door, she exclaims, "All right, the bell rang. I'd say about seventy-eight percent of people got the hint when the bell rang." There is a new seating chart this week, and as the class settles, Roberta points to an empty chair next to her. "Elijah"—she looks at a student in the third row—"move back over here."

Now with everyone's attention, Roberta reviews the agenda for the class. "Today, we're going to go to the computer lab and do something different." One student raises his hand immediately to interrupt, asking if they will be able to leave their things in the classroom. "Yes, the door will be locked," she says, but before she can continue, another student interrupts, asking if they'll need a pencil. "Yes, she replies, "but I'll tell you more about that in a minute. First, let's listen to Stardate."

Her cooperating teacher, Mr. Finn, sits at the front computer. On cue, he clicks the mouse to begin the podcast, which the class has been listening to daily since the start of the astronomy unit 2 weeks ago. The program lasts for only a few minutes, sounding crisp and clear, even from where I sit in the back of the room. Today's topic is the census of stars in our own galactic neighborhood. Students appear engaged and attentive, and some lean on their elbows to listen. A student enters with a pass, and Roberta processes it wordlessly and points him to his seat.

The podcast closes with the host's signoff, "I'm Sandy Wood." Roberta doesn't skip a beat. "Thanks, Sandy," she says. "That was fantastic." She pauses briefly before moving on. "Someone raise their hand and tell me what we did yesterday." One boy's hand shoots into the air and Roberta quickly calls on him. He says that they looked at a picture of their school and then kept shrinking the image by increasing the distance by powers of ten, "going up and up and up."

"Right," said Roberta. "The other stuff we looked at was in California, and we don't care about that, right?" Smiling at the class, she asks, "Can someone give us an idea of the kinds of things we saw?"

Students answer as they are called on. "Lakes!" says one. "Buildings!" says another. The discussion continues for another minute, and then Roberta and Mr. Finn pass out worksheets. She reminds students how their science notebooks are organized and then directs them to the precise place in their binders where the worksheets belong.

She then gives students the task of deciding which structures they think can be seen from four different vantage points in space: low-Earth orbit, the space station, the moon, and Mars. She gives an example to the class. "Who thinks they could see the continents from the moon? Put an X in the box if you think you can." Students fill in their grids quickly, but the next task—sketching what they think Earth would look like from Mars—takes a bit longer. Roberta asks if anyone needs another minute, and three students raise their hands.

She waits one more minute and then says, "While you're finishing, I'll talk a little about the computer lab. Our second step is to do a little Internet research to see if you're right." She talks to her students about the unreliability of certain websites and singles out Wikipedia in particular. "I could just go on there and write that TJ is the principal of Adams Middle School, and it would be up there." TJ, one of four African American students in the class, looks up. "He's not actually the principal, but he might be someday, right, TJ?"

"Maybe," TJ responds.

Roberta continues setting the task for the class. "We're also not going to be using Google Earth, though we will use it later on this week. Also, write down other interesting little tidbits you find. Any questions about what's expected?"

There is a pause, and then a student raises his hand. "This might be a little off topic, but . . . why doesn't our moon have a name?"

Roberta responds, "Well, it's our moon, right?"

He continues, "Well, what I mean is, Jupiter has moons, and they have names, like Io. Does our moon have a name?"

Roberta answers without pause. "That's really interesting. I don't really know. Maybe it does. Maybe you can find out and come back and tell us, because I'm interested."

A different student asks, "If you had a lot of money, could you buy the moon?"

"Actually you can buy a three-by-three plot of the moon," calls another student.

Roberta interrupts this conversation, asking if there are any more questions about the assignment. One student asks meekly, "Is the room going to be locked?"

Roberta answers as if this is the first time she's been asked. "Yes, it will be. Okay, let's make sure we're quiet in the hall. Oh, and I don't think I have to remind you—no MySpace or YouTube. Let's go."

Roberta grew up in a small industrial town with a population that was mostly White and working-class like her. In high school, she had briefly considered a career in chemical engineering, but a day spent at a Women in Engineering conference changed her mind about that. "It was just boring," she told me. "They did the typical engineering challenges, where you have to build a bridge with toothpicks, or something like that. It was just, if this is what engineers do, I don't want to do it."

Her interest in becoming a teacher began in high school, fostered by the good relationships she had formed with her own teachers. After high school, she enrolled at Delorenzo University as a chemistry major, and the choice of a career in teaching chemistry seemed natural to her from the beginning. Roberta is one of the only science teachers I know anywhere who completed the requirements for both her undergraduate degree and her teaching certification in 4 years. Given the extensive coursework and fieldwork requirements in most programs, this is no small feat.

Delorenzo University's secondary education program was 2 years long, with coursework taken by cohort and increasing fieldwork requirements each semester. Roberta had two practicum experiences her first year. Her initial placement was in a racially and ethnically diverse middle school in Delorenzo City, and her second semester placement was in a chemistry class in a suburban and largely White high school. She also fulfilled a requirement for her Teaching Diverse Learners course by serving 4 hours each week as a tutor at a Delorenzo City high school for a semester.

It was also during this semester that I had Roberta as a student in the Methods of Teaching Science course that I taught at Delorenzo University. I began this study the following year, during Roberta's third semester in the program. Though I continued to work in the Delorenzo University Secondary Science Education program and had supervisory responsibilities for a number of student teachers, Roberta was not among them.[1]

The Delorenzo University program required semester-long student teaching placements for both the third and fourth semesters. The first of these was a half-time placement, in which student teachers spent 4 hours each morning at their schools and returned to campus for afternoon coursework. Among the four teacher education programs described in this book, only Delorenzo required this component. Student teachers in these half-time placements were expected to assume full teaching responsibilities in one or two of their cooperating teacher's classes.

For this experience, Roberta was placed at South Lake High School in Delorenzo City with Mr. Calke, who had been teaching chemistry and General Science courses at the school for more than a decade. South Lake High School was relatively diverse, as shown in Table 7.1, but with slightly more White students than the district average.

For her full-time student teaching in the spring, Roberta was placed with Mr. Finn in an 8th-grade science classroom at Adams Middle School, located only a parking lot away from South Lake High School. Like few other middle school science teachers in the district, Mr. Finn had a science teaching certification rather than one in early childhood teaching. For this reason, he taught science to all of the 8th-graders in the building, and he had a reputation within the science education program at Delorenzo University as an excellent and reliable cooperating teacher. Though smaller than the high school, Adams served a similar population, as shown in Table 7.2.

From my perspective, Roberta was about as professionally supported as a student teacher could be. Both South Lake High School and Adams Middle School were part of the Professional Development School (PDS) program at Delorenzo University, a partnership between the school district, teachers' union, and university designed to support preservice teacher education by concentrating resources and student teachers at specific schools. A PDS coordinator at each school and a secondary education faculty member from Delorenzo University conducted weekly seminars with all of the schools' student teachers. Additionally, Roberta was observed three times each semester by her university supervisor—a former high school chemistry teacher himself—from whom she received detailed verbal and written feedback on her teaching. During this year of student teaching, she also met monthly with the program head, supervisors, and her cohort of science

Table 7.1. Enrollment and Race/Ethnicity Data for Roberta's Half-Time Student Teaching Placement at South Lake High School

Total Enrollment	American Indian	Asian	Black	Hispanic	White
1,928	0.7%	12.1%	21.0%	10.0%	56.3%

Table 7.2. Enrollment and Race/Ethnicity Data for Roberta's Full-Time Student Teaching Placement at Adams Middle School

Total Enrollment	American Indian	Asian	Black	Hispanic	White
478	0.0%	18.4%	14.0%	10.0%	57.5%

student teachers. Although Roberta reported being uncertain as to exactly how all of these supports facilitated her learning to teach, unlike other participants in this study, she never appeared adrift from her program or lacking in support.

〔

The course that Roberta taught in her half-time high school placement was called "ChemCom," after the popular textbook and curriculum package of the same name (American Chemical Society, 1998). As a curriculum, ChemCom focused more on the impact of chemistry on society and was considered less mathematically rigorous than other high school chemistry courses. In the Delorenzo City School District, there had been an ongoing and concerted effort to portray Chem-Com as a "science-for-nonscientists" course appropriate for college-bound students, and not as a lower-track class.

At South Lake, Roberta almost always had the opportunity to watch Mr. Calke teach a ChemCom class the period before hers. Even though they planned lessons together, Roberta reported that this follow-teaching was useful because of the way it helped her focus on what was important in the lesson. She reported that her relationship with Mr. Calke was quite positive and that she learned about tools and teaching strategies from him while strengthening her chemistry content knowledge along the way.

Although the population of her ChemCom courses largely reflected the school's demographics, the General Science course that Roberta taught later in the morning did not. The class had been designed to allow students with academic difficulties to fulfill the graduation requirement for science, and in contrast to ChemCom, there was no effort to label the course as anything other than lower track. More than half of the 21 students in Roberta's class were African American and male, and every student had an Individualized Education Plan (IEP) for accommodating his or her special needs as a learner. The classroom environment also differed significantly from the other science rooms at the school. Although ChemCom and the other chemistry classes were taught in spacious laboratory rooms, the General Science classroom was cramped and had no laboratory facilities. The implications of this arrangement did not escape Roberta's notice, as her university supervisor accurately captured in a written observation Roberta's disposition toward working with the class:

> Teaching these students under these circumstances would be challenging for any instructor, but [Roberta] has welcomed the experience and used it as an opportunity to learn more about herself and young people who come from very different and difficult backgrounds.

The initial prospect of a full-time student teaching placement in a middle school was not particularly appealing to Roberta, who fully intended to teach high school chemistry upon certification. She reported that the 8th-grade science content, which included one unit on evolution and another on planetary science, presented her with a different set of challenges compared to her prior placement:

> This semester was weird for me because I'm teaching a general eighth grade science class and I'm chemistry [certified], so I've been working with trying to teach content . . . that I haven't actually explicitly taken as coursework since I was in middle school or early high school.

Although part of her challenge was refamiliarizing herself with the content of the 8th-grade science curriculum, Roberta set herself the additional task of adapting the district's kit-based curriculum to her vision of good science teaching. Mr. Finn—who had made many adaptations himself—supported her in this effort by giving Roberta great latitude in her planning and providing her with access to a broad array of curricular resources. Throughout Roberta's full-time student teaching, he remained in the classroom and assisted her in whatever way he could without compromising her authority as a student teacher. He usually disappeared only by request.

Roberta gradually assumed responsibility for all of Mr. Finn's classes, follow-teaching for the first month and eventually taking over his five classes completely. In one post-observation conference with her university supervisor, Mr. Finn stated that he turned over his classes to her sooner than he normally does with student teachers because of his confidence in her abilities. With respect to classroom management, he noted that Roberta was one of the best student teachers he had ever mentored, and he expressed his admiration for how she was able to consistently maintain student respect and avoid unnecessary confrontation. Her planning was extensive and often went far beyond that required by the district curriculum. If she had not told me—on multiple occasions—that she was struggling with the content, I would not have known it from observing her teach.

Throughout her teacher education program, Roberta's overarching goal was getting to know and develop trusting relationships with her students, and the role this played in framing Roberta's development as a teacher cannot be understated. In a course assignment, Roberta presented the issue this way:

My students are all from very diverse backgrounds; everyone's home life and community is unique to them. I want to better use what I know about students and their lives to make their time in my classroom more fruitful and to facilitate interactions with myself and the material that is engaging for each student. When students feel that you care about them, care about what their lives are like outside of school, and that you know that it influences how they feel and act inside of school, they begin to trust you. That trust, I believe, leads to them allowing you to facilitate more personalized and engaging interactions with the material you are trying to teach them.

Whenever I went to visit Roberta's class, I saw this philosophy in action. Though Roberta herself did not frame her approach in terms of a feminist science pedagogy (Calabrese Barton, 1998; Howes, 2002), such a label describes her practice well. What was even more surprising to me was how she was able to extend these emotional bonds with her students to create connections with the content. During an introductory lesson on evolution, she spoke about how the death of Charles Darwin's daughter had affected him and his work:

When you read textbooks, you only read about the main things they did; Darwin and evolution, Einstein and relativity. But think about your life, when you're having a bad day or fight with a friend—it affects the kind of work you can do.

For Roberta, the idea that *comfort promotes learning* remained a principle of her practice throughout the study, and she applied it to both herself and her students. She saw this comfort as a precondition for motivation that ultimately facilitated science learning. She also interpreted classroom issues, such as participation in classroom activities, through the lens of student comfort. "I don't want to put students in a position where they are uncomfortable," she told me. Consequently, the solutions she brought to bear on problems of practice usually prioritized the socioemotional well-being of her students.

At the time of our first interview, Roberta had already completed a year in the Delorenzo University teacher education program. Her first semester practicum had been in a special education classroom, and Roberta told me that prior to this placement, her experience with special needs students had been very limited. She described her educational history with diversity in a similar way: "I had very little exposure to people from diverse racial backgrounds," she told me, "especially African American individuals." She said that her practicum and tutoring experiences had provided opportunities for her to interact with students from all of these backgrounds and, as a result, her comfort level had increased.

At the beginning of this study, Roberta's conceptions about diversity in general appeared to reflect the content of her previous teacher education coursework in many ways. For example, in our first interview, Roberta told me, "Individuals are more than their background," and was careful to affirm that differences were not deficiencies. She stated that her own background likely influenced her actions in the classroom as well as her interpretation of classroom events, and said that students should be held to high academic expectations regardless of their backgrounds. It was important to her that she and her students understood each other, and she expressed a desire to incorporate the lived experiences of students into the classroom because she thought that doing so would increase student motivation, engagement, and learning.

In our conversations, Roberta's conception that *individuals are more than their background* was invoked repeatedly, and she felt the Census questions on race and ethnicity provided little useful information. She noted that race and ethnicity labels did not adequately describe individual students' backgrounds, and she resisted generalizations whenever possible. She also drew attention to the significant diversity that exists within racial and ethnic categories:

> Saying that you're Asian or Latino is only one part of . . . I don't want to say genetic . . . but it's just one little part of it, and your background is so much more than this name. There's so much more culture to it that varies within the Latino community or the African American community.

Although she did acknowledge that categorical descriptions of different groups were possible, she downplayed their salience because such descriptions were not specific enough. Nonetheless, she did not deny the importance of racial, ethnic, or cultural group membership, disagreeing with the statement "I don't consider race important, I see only individual students."

There are two ways to reconcile this response with her earlier statements on individuals' backgrounds. The first interpretation is that she genuinely does see race as important, though mostly in terms of what she calls "self-identity." An alternate explanation is that she has heard the message in her coursework about the problem of "color-blindness" in teachers and does not wish to be perceived as believing that race is unimportant. In her educational philosophy, written and posted in her portfolio prior to student teaching, she noted the important role that identity groups play for students:

> Schools are diverse places full of people from different and distinct backgrounds, cultures, and varying personal dispositions. Through a student's interactions with his or her classmates, they will learn the value found in

diversity, cooperation, and collaboration. By identifying with groups within his or her peers, students create a support group for themselves for the journey to self-identity.

Besides being an outward expression of the value of diversity itself, this statement by Roberta exemplifies her equivocation between individualistic and categorical orientations to student diversity. To Roberta, diversity both mattered and did not matter,[2] and her deployment of the term *culture* is a clue to her thinking about this.

In the initial interview, as in other places throughout her written coursework from the first year of her program, Roberta depicted *culture* primarily as a set of practices and behaviors, falling just short of presenting it as an interpretive framework for perceiving the world. From her perspective, diversity was relevant because of teachers' need to understand and interpret students' practices and behaviors, yet as categorical labels they did not really communicate anything useful about individuals. In her educational philosophy, Roberta wrote that she viewed most categorical labels as arbitrary:

> Beyond classroom instruction, students should know and feel that their teacher sees them as an individual as opposed to simply a race, gender, or other arbitrary categorization. While teachers should not be "color-blind," students should know that regardless of what they look like or who they identify themselves as, their teacher has high expectations for them in terms of learning and personal conduct.

Roberta had a strong sense of the Delorenzo University teacher education program's goals, and she clearly possessed a command of the discourse in which these expectations were expressed. It is difficult therefore not to view Roberta's criticism of color-blindness as an attempt to resonate with this discourse, especially as the remainder of the paragraph might lead a reader to believe that she thinks that race and ethnicity do not have social and pedagogical implications—the very definition of "color-blindness" (Pollock, 2004; Valli, 1995).

Roberta was very aware that her perspectives might be different from those of her students. In an assignment for her Teaching Diverse Learners class, she analyzed an incident in her practicum and described the role that her own background played in these interactions. Her conclusions set a specific agenda for her forthcoming student teaching assignments:

> No matter their sociocultural background, it is impossible for students to totally compartmentalize their lives at home from their lives at school. What happens in their lives at home has a profound effect on what happens with these students in my classroom. Another dimension to this relationship is

how my presence—along with my own personal sociocultural background—changes and affects the dynamics of a classroom. My personal background colors the way in which I view how students interact with me and each other in the classroom, and it is important for me to realize this before I can begin to analyze the ways in which I interact with students in an instructional role. (Roberta's portfolio, second semester)

An example of this self-awareness could be found in Roberta's thinking about teacher-student communication. In her Teaching Diverse Learners course, she had read about "code-switching"—the linguistic concept describing the practice of moving between multiple languages or language varieties during conversation—from a reading by Lisa Delpit (2002). Roberta expressed her need to begin recognizing when her students were code-switching, and viewed it as a resource to build on.

Not being aware of one's own perspectives, in Roberta's view, had significant consequences. One of the questions in the first interview concerned a hypothetical student teacher who was observed by a supervisor to be treating her African American students in a manner different from the way she treated her White students. When I asked Roberta how she might respond in such a situation, she described her reaction in terms of one of the central messages she perceived coming from the Delorenzo teacher education program:

I would be really embarrassed, to be quite honest, but I don't know if I would necessarily admit that I was embarrassed. I'd probably end up being really defensive about it. . . . I don't know what all teacher ed programs are like, but we spend a lot of time in coursework talking about teaching diverse learners. And then the fact that you just completely blew it off when you got into the classroom—that's the surface embarrassing part, but [it's] also just really politically incorrect. [lowers voice] Oh, I'm racist now.

Her desire to avoid being labeled as a racist derived from the fact that Roberta clearly did not see herself in such a way. It also did not seem plausible to her that someone could be labeled accurately as a racist based on actions that were unintended.

Roberta also identified the need to take into account the fact that some of her students had different ways of thinking than she did. She noted that some non-White students felt that being academically successful was "acting White" and that teachers needed to counter this perception. She also worried about her ability to engage with students authentically on such issues. Roberta felt that a better way to foster student motivation and engagement occurred through caring about and connecting with students, and she viewed this type of support as essential in her teaching.

At the start of this study, Roberta's views on the pedagogical implications of student diversity centered on the relation of science content to students' lives, and she framed this connection primarily in terms of socioeconomic status. For her, incorporating the experiences of students into the curriculum reinforced the idea that students' ways of life were valued in her classroom. She felt that as a result, students would pay more attention in class, which would help them learn science more effectively.

One criticism she raised both in her coursework and in the interview concerned her perception that "multicultural education" did not focus enough on socioeconomic status. Her conception of multicultural education, at least at this point in time, was that it represented a set of strategies for targeting instruction at specific groups of students identified by categorical labels. This narrow conception of multicultural education is not uncommon among White preservice teachers (Sleeter, 2001). Addressing inequitable school cultures and structures—such as those Roberta found in her General Science class—is as much a part of multicultural education as curriculum, pedagogy, and prejudice-reduction efforts (Banks, 1995).

A portfolio entry Roberta created prior to this study drew on a specific example that demonstrated her understanding of the relationship between socioeconomics and learning science content:

> An example that comes to mind is a recent discussion I observed my cooperating teacher having with her honors chemistry class about the salt used in water softeners. The students were asked to share what they know about water softeners and how they work. I found myself, as a relatively economically disadvantaged college student, thinking, "I don't live in an apartment with a water softener! I have no idea about how they work or what they do." I can imagine that many of my students, who most likely do not live in homes with water softeners, would have had the same thoughts I did, and then lost interest in the chemistry being taught through this example.

Roberta's ability to see this example from the perspective of the learner is an indicator of her awareness of the impact of socioeconomic differences on learning. It is only a short intellectual step from this kind of thinking to active consideration of what experiences and resources students *do* have in their lives that might serve in the teaching of a concept.

For example, in the case of the water-softener lesson, a teacher might ask students if any of them have ever seen a white crusty material on the outside of a faucet or the inside of a teapot, and build the lesson around an investigation of what this substance is and where it is coming from. Knowing that it is actually calcium carbonate would help her to guide her students' explorations in ways that could lead toward a deeper understanding of the behavior of ions in solution.

Although Roberta felt that teachers should use examples drawn from experiences familiar to their students, it was much more difficult for Roberta to articulate examples connected to race, ethnicity, and culture. For example, I asked her how she might respond to a student who asked if sulfur bonds form only in White people's hair. Though unsure of the answer, she saw such a question as a "jumping-off point" for further class investigation. When I asked how the racial or ethnic composition of the class might affect her response, she had more difficulty in answering, and conveyed uncertainty about what might motivate such a question in the first place:

> It depends on . . . the race and ethnicity I guess—I don't want to say percentages. . . . If your class is mostly White students and you have, like, one or two African American students—I mean, cultural relevance goes both ways. But you don't want to discount what they're saying and it's interesting to think about. . . . I guess I don't know why an African American student would care necessarily [about] the chemistry or the bonding behind curly-haired people, and White people the other way around, know what I mean?

In expressing her belief that cultural relevance goes "both ways," Roberta is depicting a zero-sum image of culturally relevant pedagogy; she perceives that content relevant to one group will not necessarily be relevant to another. The task she sees before her as a teacher is to devise a curriculum that is relevant for all students. Fundamentally, this is no different from her earlier water-softener example, in that students either come from homes with water softeners or they don't. Yet race is different for her in the sense that she does not appear to have the same easy access to examples as she does for content that might better relate to different socioeconomic levels.

Ultimately, Roberta did learn about her students' lives. Making sense of what she found, however, turned out to be much more difficult than she anticipated. Over the course of the year, Roberta made a sustained effort to get to know her students, and there is much evidence that she developed trusting relationships with many of them. As I sifted through all of the data I had collected about Roberta's case, I had expected to find that Roberta's intention to learn about her students' lives would bring her insights about the ways in which race and ethnicity still mattered in schooling. I reasoned, how could it not?

The most straightforward way to characterize the changes in Roberta's conceptions about the pedagogical implications of student diversity is that she became even more convinced over time that race and ethnicity had, for all practical purposes, *no* pedagogical implications. This belief was clearly reinforced by her desire to see her students as individuals.

In later interviews, Roberta echoed her earlier response to the hair chemistry question, saying that she did not know the differences between White and African American hair but would certainly look it up and get back to the student. Such a question did not actually seem realistic to her. By the completion of her student teaching, her answer shifted the focus of the conversation away from race and toward gender:

> You know, I don't particularly know the answer, and I'd tell them that. And then I'd try and find out, because it's an interesting thing. . . . I think that, especially for girls that age, their hair is a really big deal—I know, I was one. And whether you're White or African American or anything else, your hair is important to you, and I think that would be an interesting study.

In other words, Roberta could identify how girls' interest in their hair could serve the purpose of learning more science, but making a similar claim about the interests of her African American students was much more difficult.

The idea that the social category of race might have relevance in teaching science remained farfetched to Roberta, even when it held explanatory power. Over the course of her two semesters of student teaching, there were times when evidence appeared to point to race as a mitigating factor in students' school experiences, yet Roberta remained hesitant to invoke racism as part of the explanation. This remained true even as she smoldered about the indignities suffered by her students, two of which I share here.

The first example concerned both the demographic composition of her General Science class as well as the substandard room to which she and her students were assigned. In her descriptions of this situation, Roberta chose not to use race labels, despite the fact the students in her class were overwhelmingly African American. She chose instead to use the more generic term "at risk," which Ladson-Billings notes often serves as a proxy label for race (1999, p. 218). Framing this situation as one of lowered expectations, she made it very clear to me in our discussions—and to the readers of her portfolio—that this situation represented a stinging injustice:

> I feel as if this particular room assignment for this particular group of students says a lot about the way the school values these students—both as

individuals and as learners of science. By putting them in this classroom, the school is essentially telling them that the "powers that be" do not believe they are capable of learning science. If they are not capable of learning science, why waste resources on them?

Roberta recognized the effect of lowered expectations for these students, but still could not bring the analytic lens of race to bear on this situation, even when pressed.

I wondered why was it so difficult for her to ask similar questions about the disproportionate representation of African American students labeled "at risk." One hint came during her half-time teaching experience, as we discussed a recently published series of news articles concerning the disparity between White and Black students in the district's high school dropout rate. In the year prior, state data reports showed that White students at South Lake High School had a 3% dropout rate, while the rate for African American students was 28%. This issue was bewildering to Roberta on a number of levels, and she struggled to reconcile such statistics with her experiences at the school:

I am trained to think about data and draw conclusions from data. But my personal experience sometimes says different, and that's what's hard for me. Because I don't look at kids and think, "You're not going to graduate." So that's what's been really hard for me, because the data tells me that there is a correlation—whatever the theories are, why students . . . who are African American, Latino-Latina, or of Asian descent don't do as well as Caucasian students—there's a bunch of theories out there . . . but it's so hard for me to make the connection. . . . As a teacher, I can't look at a kid and think "You're not going to graduate, you're not going to do this," cause why am I here? So that's so hard for me to do, to make that bridge between analyzing data, and how I know kids.

In fact, it appeared that much of her previous attention to what the "bunch of theories" said about the social context of schooling had subsided. The following list of questionnaire statements were items she was neutral toward or disagreed with in September at the start of her half-time student teaching but agreed with in June at the completion of full-time student teaching. That is, all of the following became *more plausible* to Roberta over the course of her year of student teaching:

- I don't consider race important; I see only individual students.
- If a student works hard, he or she can achieve academic excellence regardless of his or her race, ethnicity, or culture.
- It is not proper for teachers to use racial descriptors (Black, Latino, etc.) when talking with other teachers about students.

All of these statements point toward an overall decline in a belief about the salience of race in schooling. Instead, building from her earlier concept that individuals matter more than does their background, she grew more certain that schooling represented a place where issues of race played no role. Or at least, as the next example shows, where race *ought* to play no role.

During her full-time middle school placement, Roberta noticed that the students who were continually restricted from going on field trips were almost all African American students. In fact, the school kept a written record, known informally as the "no-go list," for the purpose of restricting students from trips. In describing the no-go list, Roberta talked about her difficulty in coming to terms with the role that race played:

> I always think about that list of the kids who can't go. This thing's based on behavior, and it's all behavior and not academic. It's always the African American students. . . . There was one Latina girl that couldn't go to one—other than that it's always the same group of African American students. . . . I think about it a lot, actually. Why this particular group of students? I don't have a lot of problems with these particular kids, but I hear about problems that other teachers have with them, that they get sent out, and they get misconducts, and that's why they don't get to go on these trips. And I just wonder about it a lot.

To Roberta, the fact that her relationships with students on the no-go list might be stronger than were those of other teachers is one possibility that might explain the no-go list being disproportionately Black. However, this would make sense only if the other teachers were racist, which she did not believe. For the first time—at the end of her program—Roberta suggested some other factors that she thought might point toward a different explanation:

> I think about the criteria for what makes the no-go list. Like . . . getting misconducts and not having any suspensions and having too many tardies and things like that. And I think about why might a kid be tardy to school every day. Like, what's going on at home that this kid can't get to school on time every day? And because of that they're not allowed to go on this trip. Or, if there's one particular teacher that this kid just doesn't get along with and they get sent out all the time and they get misconducts, that gets built up and they can't go on this trip, even though they might be delightful in other classes. And you just think about how all these things lead to them having documented behavior issues that have consequences for them.

It is evident that Roberta had expanded her thinking about the effect of social context on her students' school lives and had even identified mechanisms by which this might happen. Yet an explicit connection between the racialized nature of this social context and its operation in schools still appeared to be beyond her grasp.

Such a connection requires thinking in terms of probability rather than strict causality. In the United States the likelihood that a student is poor increases if he or she is African American, and the reasons why are well known. Many have documented how public policy issues relating to jobs, transportation, and housing have a disproportionately negative impact on schooling for poor students and students of color in the United States (Anyon, 2005; Kozol, 1991, 2005). A schooling sanction, such as being on a no-go list, is simply more likely for African American students because of the higher probability that the institutional and historical effects of racism have come into play.

There was another unexpected factor in Roberta's interpretations of these situations, however. I could not decide if Roberta was unable or simply unwilling to draw on knowledge gained in her coursework about institutional racism to explain the patterns she had identified. Upon digging further, I was unable to find any evidence in my data that Roberta had grasped the nature and operation of racism at *any* point in her program. In Roberta's case, these data sources included four interviews, field notes from four teaching observations, six written supervisor observations, a detailed and comprehensive reflective portfolio, and three very long questionnaires. Even the "Teaching Story Analysis" written for her Teaching Diverse Learners class held no evidence that the concept of racism was clear to her, other than the fact that it was undesirable to be labeled as a racist.

Needless to say, this came as something of a surprise to me, given all of the attention paid to race in Roberta's coursework and fieldwork. Apparently, she had successfully avoided engagement in the issue of racism over her 2 years in the program, and even knowing her well, it was something even I had not noticed.

Roberta reported hearing repeatedly in her program that *teachers must learn about their students' lives*. Although the teacher educators in Roberta's program may have intended that the influence of race on students' lives be an integral part of this knowledge, Roberta's individualistic orientation toward student diversity ensured that it did not. Without this framework for understanding how race operates in a social context, constructing explanations for racialized patterns in schools was a difficult task indeed.

◻

The set of leveled readings and graphic organizers that Roberta developed for her 3-week unit on evolution during her 8th grade placement was one of the more remarkable pieces of curriculum development by a student teacher that I have ever seen. Mr. Finn was similarly impressed and described it as one of the highlights of his year. In designing this unit, Roberta clearly saw that the cultural backgrounds of her students had pedagogical implications, as she wrote in her portfolio:

> When the topic of evolution is brought up, creationism and intelligent design are also bound to come up. As an instructor of science, I feel that it is counterproductive to pretend that views based in creationism/intelligent design do not exist. The science classroom is populated with students from all different religious and cultural backgrounds; that very fact makes addressing non-scientific views on how we came to be the way we are essential.

In introducing the unit to her class, Roberta reassured students that their beliefs need not conflict with learning about evolution:

> No one—not your school, not your teacher, not your peers, not your friends— has the right to tell you what to believe. However, when you come through the door to my science classroom, I see you as scientists. It is my job to help you to learn how to think like a scientist, so it is my right to tell you what you need to know. What you believe and what you know do not have to be the same thing.

Such a statement was consistent with Roberta's desire to create an emotionally safe classroom, and by positioning her students as scientists, she was also reinforcing the high expectations she had for them. Unlike in some U.S. classrooms, where such a statement precedes an impoverished presentation of the concepts of evolution (Berkman, Pacheco, & Plutzer, 2008), Roberta's depiction of evolutionary content over the next 3 weeks was conceptually strong and aligned with state and national science education standards (National Research Council, 1996).

The pedagogical implications of culture for Roberta in this unit related primarily to language. She believed that by making distinctions between scientific and nonscientific language, such as in the use of the word "theory," she would also be encouraging her students to make distinctions between scientific and nonscientific ways of viewing the world.

Roberta was universally praised by her instructors, cooperating teachers, and university supervisor as an exemplary student teacher. She was able to hone her craft in the classrooms of Mr. Calke and Mr. Finn as she encountered new ideas, developed her management skills, and strengthened her content knowledge. Her classroom activities kept students active and interested within a content-rich environment, and she attended closely to her students' socioemotional needs.

These qualities were all illustrated in Roberta's work with students labeled as English language learners (ELLs), which was singled out by both her supervisor and cooperating teacher as exemplary. Roberta herself reported that she had not worked with ELL students at all until her full-time student teaching. She became aware of a range of strategies for working with ELL students through contact with support personnel and professional development resources at the school, and worked to incorporate this new knowledge into her classroom. Much of what she learned, such as the importance of scaffolding scientific language for English language learners, was consistent with what she already believed about good science teaching.

Over time, Roberta sensed that her ELL students were not having the same positive experiences in science class as her other students were. By the end of student teaching, Roberta still described her ELL teaching as inadequate and indicated a need to learn more about specifically teaching science to this population of students. In discussing this with me, she deployed the concept of culture in a manner she previously had not:

I think sometimes cultural views of science are different from where you are. . . . Maybe not so much Latino and Latina students, but students who are Hmong have a different view. . . . The western view of science is that . . . technology and globalization [have] been a really good thing. And those students, their view may be that's not such a good thing.

In this passage Roberta has identified a potential source of conflict for her Hmong students based on perceptions framed by culture, and she recognizes that this view is at odds with science as commonly presented in schools. She told me that she had been led to this idea by conversations with particular students as well as from an article in *The Science Teacher* magazine (Edmonds, 2009). In a written reflection about this article for her portfolio, she described the implications of her newfound idea that culture informs the ways in which students view science itself:

Getting to know the ways in which my students' cultural backgrounds shape the way they know and view science will help me to interpret how that cultural lens works as a force in my classroom. . . . Inquiring into what my students value—and how that affects their view of science—sends the message that I value their ways of knowing and that I believe it has intellectual value. Equally as important, knowing what my students themselves already know helps me, as an instructor, to develop learning goals and appropriate instructional activities that help students use their cultural knowledge to build bridges to understanding modern Western explanations and interpretations of scientific phenomena. (Roberta's portfolio, fourth semester)

Although the identification of the salience of culture for science learning is promising on the one hand, Roberta's writing here is reminiscent of her earlier work in the Teaching Diverse Learners course in that it aligns very well with what her university supervisor and others in her teacher education program might like to hear. Yet this understanding may prove more durable because of the self-directed nature of her learning. This reframing of the concept of culture was also situated in an attempt to solve a problem of practice that she had identified, something that is known to foster teacher learning (Bell & Gilbert, 1996).

In the summer after graduation, Roberta focused her job search efforts in Briggstown, but on the day before school started in September, she received a surprise offer for a chemistry teaching position in the Delorenzo City School District and was assigned two different courses. The first was a traditional college preparatory chemistry course, and when we talked again just before winter break, she volunteered the information (knowing that I would ask, she told me) that the students in it were "ninety-eight percent White." The other course, which she described as being similar to the ChemCom course she had taught during half-time student teaching, was simply called General Chemistry, and had a much more diverse student body. Certain that there was "some mechanism for how it got that way," she was still unsure how to explain the racial imbalances in her two courses.

After reading an earlier draft of the case, which Roberta said, "rings true for the most part," she defended her approach to addressing student diversity. "Treating students as individuals and letting them know I treat them as individuals—that's what I do in the classroom. This is just where I am right now."

We talked about the issue I had noted concerning her difficulty in understanding how institutional racism affects individual students. "It's hard to bridge that gap," she said, "but I know in the back of my head it's still there." Roberta indicated that for her, it was easier to focus on institutional racism in the first year of her teacher education program because it had seemed more generalized. She noted that once she began to form substantive relationships with students during student teaching, it simply became harder to apply what she had learned about institutional discrimination in explaining the difficulties her individual students faced.

I asked her if she felt that teachers ought to raise questions in possible cases of institutional discrimination, and pointed to the absence of students of color in her college prep chemistry classes as an example. Roberta's response reminded me that throughout this study her moral obligations had always been directed toward her students as individuals, where, perhaps, she saw her chances of success as greatest:

> I don't run the school. Yes, it's important to understand how the school works, but at the end of the day, I have thirty students in each class I have to teach. My concern is, how can I make their experience more meaningful? What can I by myself do?

CHAPTER 8

Conclusion

Drawing the Map of Learning to Teach

> A basic tenet of education is that instruction should follow development. Yet we have no maps of how teacher cognitions, beliefs and skills with respect to the teaching of diverse student populations actually develop. We do not know what a beginning teacher really knows versus what successful, experienced colleagues might know about the teaching of diverse student populations. If we could map how teachers move from the former to the latter, we might be able to plan teacher education programs to help teachers better develop these skills.
>
> —Grant & Secada, 1990, p. 419

Each case in this book may be thought of as a single photon on a photographic plate—or a single pixel on a screen—that begins to reveal the map that Grant and Secada envisioned. Our map allows us to point to a common destination, which in this study means becoming an excellent science teacher who is able to teach diverse student populations in a way that fosters a deep and enduring understanding of scientific concepts and practices. This emerging map is necessarily incomplete, but in this final chapter I would like to sketch the contours of the terrain coming into view.

There is growing consensus in the field of science education about good science teaching, in terms of both curricular content and pedagogy (National Research Council, 2012). It is vital that science teacher education programs engage with this vision—critiquing it, as necessary—because some of the practices being advocated have existed previously only on the margins of traditional high school science teaching. These promising practices include having students develop and deploy explanatory models; argue claims based on evidence; and search for, evaluate, and communicate scientific information in the same ways that practicing scientists do.

This vision also includes explicit attention to equity and foregrounds the goal of equalized opportunities to learn. It requires the creation of inclusive classrooms that build on students' prior understandings and draw on cultural funds of knowledge and patterns of communication to foster deep and lasting learning (González, Moll, & Amanti, 2005). In these diverse science classrooms, the vision of good teaching also entails consideration of the social, cultural, and cognitive contexts within which student ideas are understood. James Banks once described a *multicultural atom* as an atom that all kids can understand (in Tucker, 1998), but in many classrooms such atoms are rare elements indeed because of the way that science is presented to students.

When scientific knowledge is portrayed as content to be transmitted—or wisdom to be received—it feeds into the belief that there is only one acceptable and official form of knowledge (Apple, 2000; Banks, 1995). Although the accumulated wisdom of science is indeed impressive, and scientific uncertainty has to be distinguished from genuine ignorance, the authority for this knowledge comes from a robust understanding of how it came to be (Ladson-Billings, 1994; Rudolph, 2007). This is an all-too-uncommon aspect of science classrooms today, where many students still see the steady accumulation of factual knowledge as the goal. There is much to be gained by focusing the attention of prospective teachers on cultivating the habits of mind that allow them to carefully examine linkages between their teaching and students' learning.

Though the coordinates of the "excellent science teacher" destination on the map are becoming increasingly clear, there are less desirable locations elsewhere that will likely continue to attract travelers for the foreseeable future. One of them is a land of activities, where interesting hands-on tasks keep students engaged but with little prospect of robust science learning. Another is a country of routines, where classroom management concerns and textbook chapters trump authentic engagement with learners' ideas. The last and perhaps most alarming destination is the one that looks just like the ideal, except that it is segregated along lines of privilege.

Making good use of our map also depends on knowing how prospective teachers have packed for their journeys, and how the tools, abilities, and previous life experiences that they carry will help them along the way. For example, Armando's personal understanding of the lived experiences of race meant covering familiar ground when it came to understanding systemic discrimination. This terrain proved to be a long, hard slog for others: consider Kathy's response to racist student behavior and Roberta's difficulty in understanding the racialized nature of graduation rates at her school.

The metaphor of the map also supports the notion that individual travelers have different starting points and are not limited to a single pathway for their respective journeys. I refer not to "pathways into teaching" that describe various routes or program features that lead to certification (e.g. Boyd et al., 2006), but to the conceptual pathways, sometimes called "learning progressions," that individuals follow as they develop understandings during the process of learning to teach (Fuller, 1969; Thompson, Braaten, & Windschitl, 2009). These different tracks might lead some teachers easily over certain obstacles, whereas others might need to take a longer way around.

A few other areas on the map are worth further contemplation if we are to fully take stock of the territory covered in this research. Some are well-known landmarks in teacher education, but others make unexpected appearances, and deserve to be better known features of this topography.

LANDMARK #1: CONCEPTUAL PARALLELS

During the course of this study, a number of striking similarities appeared among the ways individuals thought about particular conceptions in ostensibly separate domains. I call these *conceptual parallels* here in order to suggest that thinking in these domains is somehow connected to a dominant organizing conception within a person's conceptual ecology. I give three examples of these conceptual parallels here, and describe the ways in which these seemed to be connected to other elements within a broader conceptual ecology.

Sources of Motivation

For some in this study, ideas concerning classroom management were linked to a vision of student learning driven almost wholly by external motivations. Tyler, Jethro, Kathy, and Roberta used behavioral reinforcements to varying extents as a regular part of their teaching practice to manage the class environment as well as to confer approval when students arrived at correct answers in classroom and laboratory activities. Such strategies have a long history in the practices of schooling and are aptly described by Kohn's (1993) label of "pop-behaviorism," which he defines as the practice of doling out rewards and punishments to influence behavior.

What was interesting was that some of these teachers considered "right answers" themselves—particularly in tasks and lab activities—to be external positive reinforcements on student motivation. For example, Jethro considered a successful experiment to be a reward that increased motivation, whereas a "failed" experiment was interpreted as a punishment that decreased motivation. This is not how scientists generally think about their experimental work. In fact, it is more common to read accounts of failed experiments that actually increased researchers' desire to search for answers with further experimentation (e.g., Collins & Pinch, 1998). Yet to Jethro, external motivation was a pressure that needed to be constantly maintained, without which the fragile edifice of student engagement would collapse entirely.

Inquiry and Knowledge

In all of the cases, there were similarities in the ways individuals thought about the meaning of "inquiry" in different situations. The conception regarding the nature of knowledge held by each individual appeared to be similarly expressed across a variety of circumstances, including their portrayals of how scientific knowledge is generated, descriptions of student learning in laboratory activities in class, and in acts of setting and solving issues related to their own practice.

Tyler treated knowledge as the sum of a steady accumulation of facts in both biology and his teaching, and saw knowledge itself as unproblematic, almost as a currency to be exchanged (Freire, 1970; Smith, Maclin, Houghton, & Hennessey, 2000). He viewed the knowledge he gained in his teacher preparation program in the same way. Conversely, Corrine and Armando, both of whom had extensive experience in science laboratories and possessed a sophisticated understanding of the role of evidence in knowledge claims, often questioned their own assumptions and others' assertions about teaching. They also attended more to evidence when being reflective about their own practice. Neither was satisfied with their attempts to implement inquiry approaches to learning in their own classrooms. As described in his case, Jethro's conceptions about scientific inquiry were somewhat haphazard and were reflected in his content, his pedagogy, and in his approach to inquiring about his own teaching.

Conflict Avoidance

The fear of unexpected professional repercussions, which Tyler expressed openly, seemed a driving force in many of these stories. During the course of this study, most participants noted that certain things that they did or said in the classroom—relating to evolution, race, politics, and school equity issues—could potentially get them in trouble with parents, administrators, or their fellow teachers.

There were also times when the student teachers in this study intentionally avoided conflict with students, and these instances seemed to occur mostly when the consequences of engaging in conflict were uncertain. When outcomes were more predictable—for example when cooperating teachers were involved in some way—there seemed little hesitancy to engage in conflict, particularly in classroom management situations.

Of course, avoiding escalation in such circumstances is often appropriate, but conflict itself is not always a bad thing. Kathy arguably ought to have initiated conflict with the student who drew the racist caricatures. Even academically, the act of pressing students for further explanation represents a situation in which conflict between a persistent teacher and a resistant student may be quite productive.

The understanding that conflict may be productive—and is in fact necessary for democratic cultures to thrive—may be counterintuitive, especially to new teachers who may view conflict through the lens of pop-behaviorism described earlier. Whether pressing students for evidence to support an idea, confronting racist behavior in the classroom, or advocating for equitable school structures, the ability to engage in productive conflict across a wide variety of settings is a skill new teachers clearly must learn.

LANDMARK #2:
THE EXPERIENCE OF STUDENT TEACHING

It was surprising to see how strongly cooperating teachers' ideas about learning to teach appeared to play a role in their student teachers' experiences. Most of them considered student teaching a time for student teachers to just jump right in and begin teaching. With the exceptions of Mr. Calke and Mr. Finn, who both appeared to a have a genuine master/apprentice relationship with Roberta, most of the cooperating teachers provided little supervision and minimal feedback on the day-to-day activities of their student teachers; they essentially handed over their classes. I wish to be fair to the cooperating teachers, who no doubt felt that they were doing their student teachers a favor by granting them so much autonomy. Like a ship's captain who returns to the bridge to ensure safe passage in the proper direction, they never completely relinquished control and were usually on hand to help out whenever problems arose. Many of them took on other professional responsibilities while their student teachers taught, but more often than not they could be found grading papers in an adjoining science prep room. The laissez-faire approach taken by most cooperating teachers in this study ought not to be taken as an abdication of responsibilities but rather as a rational judgment call on the best use of their time. My own assessment, however, is that these practices offer little benefit to student teachers, at least compared to receiving ongoing feedback that engages both their daily practice and ideas about teaching.

Unquestionably, the classroom experiences of the student teachers did provide them with opportunities to learn. When ideas about the pedagogical implications of student diversity changed in this study, it was most often a consequence of attempting to address a problem of practice in the classroom. Tyler's focus on grading accurately led him to identify certain differences in communication styles between his White and Black students. Roberta's struggles with her English language learners led her to acknowledge the different views of science held by her Hmong students. Armando's recognition of the disparate demands made on his African American students' cognitive skills in different environments was linked to the frustration he felt from the lowered student expectations of his practicum group. In each of these cases, participants drew on the resources provided by their teacher education coursework in order to inform their responses to placement-specific situations.

Content knowledge played a key role in this learning. Simply put, when individuals improved their understanding of particular science topics, they were better able to identify potential opportunities for multicultural content integration. Tyler's sickle-cell anemia example and Roberta's careful development of her evolution unit perhaps represent this best.

The role of time in mediating participants' ability to engage in reflective practice about their teaching was also a salient factor in determining what and how the participants in this study learned to teach. The SAMTEP program at Briggstown was time-intensive, compressing a great deal of coursework into a single year. Prospective teachers took classes three nights each week throughout each semester and as a result were left with little time to reflect about their ongoing experiences.

It is worth noting that the Briggstown and Delorenzo programs each allotted programmatic time based on their respective values and visions of good teaching. The Delorenzo program emphasized reflective practice, and the completion of the portfolio during the full-time teaching semester was favored over compressing the time frame of the program. The Briggstown program, however, considered it more important to get capable and willing individuals certified quickly, given the number of science teacher vacancies in the metropolitan area. Clearly, these programmatic orientations had an effect on individuals' opportunity to learn across multiple dimensions, not just in terms of being prepared to teach for diversity.

LANDMARK #3: PROBABILISTIC THINKING

I did not begin this research thinking much about individuals' capacity to engage in probabilistic thinking—the cognitive ability to estimate the likelihood of possible events. Yet during the course of this study, this ability emerged as an important factor that directly affected participants' ability to teach science in diverse classrooms.

If difficulty with engaging in probabilistic thinking was related only to subject matter, it would likely be of little concern here, taking its place among the other areas of content knowledge in which prospective teachers might demonstrate a lack of mastery. Yet the inability of student teachers in this study to speak in terms of probabilities concerning genetic crosses and locations of electrons was an initial clue that this sort of thinking posed certain difficulties for them.

As even the most casual observer of games of chance knows, understanding the probability of a particular event in a given situation is an element in expertise. Novices tend to rely more on specific data they receive about a probabilistic situation and ignore other information, even if it is more logical or well established (Nickerson, 2004). For example, if an unbiased coin comes up heads on the first three tosses, the novice might predict that the next one will probably be heads also, whereas the expert knows it is just as likely to come up tails no matter what the previous results. It is also cognitively more difficult to construct mental models in probabilistic terms when there are multiple variables, a condition that almost always applies to teaching situations. The contexts and reference points for these calculations also matter a great deal (Kahneman, 2011), as I now demonstrate in three different aspects of teacher learning in this study.

Probabilistic Thinking About the Pedagogical Implications of Student Diversity

A recurring theme across the stories of the White student teachers in this study was the dilemma over what to do with stereotypes. On the one hand, many felt that categorical differences were negligible given that every individual is unique, and considered stereotypes both simplistic and discriminatory. On the other, they desperately desired to have some way to speak about groups of students in a generalized manner. When it came to gender, it was not difficult for them simply to talk about differences in girls and boys. When it came to race, ethnicity, and culture however, most of the White teachers considered speaking categorically about students to be inappropriate or even potentially threatening.

Interestingly, Armando—the one person of color in this study—was able to speak probabilistically about his students where most of his peers were not. "Stereotypes exist for a reason, and I don't think they're bad things, necessarily," Armando told me. "Where the gulf exists between stereotypes and reality is that we don't give people lease to be individuals within them." As shown in his case, Tyler had also come to a similar conclusion by the completion of his student teaching.

There were times when individuals clearly engaged in probabilistic thinking, such as when I asked Corrine why a White teacher in a hypothetical scenario might have negative interactions with her African American students. She responded:

> Well, given the fact that she's in a small Midwestern town, it's likely that she's uncomfortable with African American population. Probably not a whole lot of exposure, or she may even have a negative opinion of that race of people.

Compare this with her apparent difficulty in making a probabilistic statement about her students of color:

> Just in general there seems to be a . . . I don't know how to put this . . . White students have a different cultural upbringing in terms of what school is required for, than students of color in some regards. Not necessarily, it doesn't hold true across the board, but statistically African American and Latino cultures don't place as high a value on education as White[s] do.

What is interesting here is the possibility that probabilistic thinking about a member of an *in-group* (Allport, 1979) might not be as difficult as probabilistic thinking about other groups. Like the hypothetical teacher in the scenario, Corrine is White, female, and from the Midwestern United States, so perhaps it is easier for her to compute probabilities for someone she perceives to be like herself.

Probabilistic Thinking and the Problem of Enactment

Essentially, the problem of enactment can be described as knowing what to do but not knowing how to do it; it has been identified as one of the central problems of learning to teach (Hammerness et al., 2005; Kennedy, 1998). The problem of enactment occurs when a prediction, derived from a conception about teaching, meets the context in which it is to be enacted. The ability to make a prediction about one's teaching in a given context requires being able to think probabilistically. Taleb (2007) draws on the ideas of Dennett (2003) to describe the predictive aspects of probabilistic thinking in this way:

> What is the most potent use of our brain? It is precisely the ability to project conjectures into the future and play the counterfactual game—"If I punch him in the nose, then he will punch me back right away, or, worse, call his lawyer in New York." One of the advantages of doing so is that we can let our conjectures die in our stead. Used correctly and in place of more visceral reactions, the ability to project effectively frees us from immediate, first-order natural selection—as opposed to more primitive organisms that were vulnerable to death and only grew by improvement in the gene pool through selection of the best. In a way, projecting allows us to cheat evolution: it now takes place in our head, as a series of projections and counterfactual scenarios. (p. 188)

In a discussion about why it is sometimes hard to put into practice something she knows is "right to do," Corrine described the difficulty of predicting how a lesson will unfold:

> There have been times when I'm up there and I'm planning this thing and I'm like, "Let's just skip that part . . . now that I'm here and I'm thinking about it. Out there, this is how I envisioned it going. Standing here, in front of you all—no, that's not going to work."

Part of the enactment problem then relates to the predictive aspects of probabilistic thinking. If probabilistic thinking is difficult for preservice teachers, it follows, from this view at least, that enactment will be a difficult task.

Probabilistic Thinking in Teacher Education

As I watched the teachers in this study, I often thought they would benefit from a strategy offered by Grant and Sleeter (2007): "We use demographic characteristics to alert us to the diversity of the class, then listen carefully to students themselves to figure out what their diversity might mean" (pp. 48–49). I think teacher educators have underestimated the difficulty of this approach, and not just for White preservice teachers.

Teachers need to be able to continually gather data on their students to assess the likelihood that their students will have had certain life experiences or hold particular ideas. New teachers may resist doing this because they think it is stereotyping, but estimating how many students might have faced institutional discrimination in past science classes is functionally no different from figuring out how many might have a misconception about an upcoming science topic. Both require estimates of probability that ought to influence a teacher's planning and pedagogy. Teacher educators can help teachers to gather contextual information about their students to slowly replace stereotypes, and work with them to consider probabilities about what students are bringing to the classroom in terms of their life histories as well as their prior conceptions about science.

The link between thinking probabilistically and engaging in reflection about one's practice is a logical one to make. Prospective teachers need opportunities to consider the multiple ways a given classroom situation might have unfolded and how different actions on their part might have led to different outcomes. Teacher educators can support this process by encouraging their preservice teachers to generate multiple approaches to the problems of practice and by pushing them to consider the range of potential outcomes when using various teaching approaches. It is also a good idea to model the use of probabilistic language when speaking about students categorically. Both approaches help scaffold the important task of helping prospective teachers learn to reframe problems of practice.

LANDMARK #4: RETHINKING MODELS
OF TEACHER KNOWLEDGE

It has been a generation since Shulman (1986, 1987) introduced and made distinctions between the different types of knowledge needed for teaching. *Content knowledge* and *pedagogical knowledge* are Shulman's pillars that support the notion of *pedagogical content knowledge*, the specialized form of teacher knowledge that informs how teachers help students learn particular content. Since that time, other scholars have enriched and expanded on these ideas to create rich models of knowledge for teaching (e.g. Ball, Thames, & Phelps, 2008; Cochran-Smith & Lytle, 2009). Although Shulman's categorizations have been undoubtedly productive in helping to depict what teachers *ought* to know, they may not adequately account for how teachers themselves have organized their own knowledge for teaching (and have constructed their own maps of learning to teach).

The identification of "conceptual parallels" in this study troubles such models of teacher knowledge because it suggests the importance of teachers' conceptions about knowledge, their affective preferences, and their other ways of organizing knowledge for teaching. Handal & Lauvas (1987) portray such practitioner-centered models of knowledge as teachers' *practical theories*, and claim these are the main determining factors in teachers' practice. Shulman's categories may indeed represent useful ways for the disciplinary field of education to organize knowledge, but if we are to talk about how this knowledge changes for individuals over time, the model of a conceptual ecology appears better suited to the task.

It is perhaps an artifact of institutions of higher education, where knowledge is divided up into areas of expertise across disciplines (into which prospective teachers are then organized), that we often cut our activities along Shulman's seams in teacher preparation programs. Yet there is no reason why prospective teachers' own prior knowledge, personal goals, and conceptions about teaching cannot also be made objects of study. When teachers interrogate their own ideas, they also develop their abilities to reframe their problems of practice; they are better able to step outside the narrow boundaries of their own common sense and access different ways of thinking about their teaching to identify new solutions to their problems.

When teachers are able to inform this process of reframing by tapping into the rich knowledge about teaching and learning, they are essentially overlaying their own map of learning to teach with ours, and the results can be powerful indeed. I think that this ability to draw upon available resources and reframe problems of practice is the main distinction between teachers who are well prepared and those who are not.

LOOKING UPON THE INTERNAL

My arguments in this book rest on the assumption that teachers ought to be active intellectuals and agents of change toward a more just society (Zeichner, 2009). This is not a universally shared view, particularly in our age of standardized tests, high-stakes teacher evaluations, and attacks on teachers as unaccountable and incompetent public employees. It is my belief that teachers ought to be prepared both as professionals with specialized knowledge and as engaged stakeholders in a democracy. The health of human societies, and perhaps our own future as a species, depends on equitable access to both scientific knowledge and its fruits. Science teachers certainly have a strong role to play in shaping this future.

Preparing teachers to teach science for understanding is as important as preparing teachers for the diversity of the modern classroom, and these goals need not be mutually exclusive. More than a century ago, educational philosopher John Dewey (1904) wrote about the importance of focusing on what he termed the "mental movement" of the student, and it is illuminating to read his words today with teachers in diverse science classrooms in mind:

> Only by beginning with the values and laws contained in the student's own experience of his own mental growth, and by proceeding gradually to facts connected with other persons of whom he can know little; and by proceeding still more gradually to the attempt actually to influence the mental operations of others, can educational theory be made most effective. Only in this way can the most essential trait of the mental habit of the teacher be secured — that habit which looks upon the internal, not upon the external; which sees that the important function of the teacher is direction of the mental movement of the student, and that the mental movement must be known before it can be directed. (1904/2008, p. 793)

From the perspective of teaching science for understanding, the capacity to ascertain and act upon student thinking is the only way to ensure that deep and lasting learning is occurring. From the perspective of teaching in diverse classrooms, it is the practice of looking "upon the internal" that gives teachers insight into the experiences that shape the understandings students hold about the world. Science education as a field has a strong tradition of focusing on the ideas of learners, and we now leverage this history to create more powerful opportunities for teacher learning.

It has been my position throughout this research that student ideas constitute the raw material of teachers' work. Teachers must be able to sense the manner in which they are working with this raw material, much like a potter must be able to see and feel the clay. A clear perception of how students' ideas are affected by experiences in the classroom can lead to powerful and effective instruction, the key finding from decades of work on assessment and feedback in classrooms (Atkin, 2005; Black & Wiliam, 1998; Hattie & Timperley, 2007).

I argue now, as have others before me, that this outlook is just as important for teacher educators working with prospective teachers as it is for prospective teachers and their pupils (Hewson, 1992; Russell & Martin, 2007). Teacher educators must take into account their prospective teachers' ideas about teaching, learning, subject matter, schools, society, and diversity if these are to be the areas on which we focus during teacher preparation. Dewey's suggestion also holds for teachers and teacher educators when they turn their attention inward to examine their own values and laws, intentionally directing their own mental movement as they grow and learn as educators.

Attending to student thinking is no easy task for new teachers, and it is an added challenge in classrooms where teachers and students do not share each other's cultural perspectives and life experiences. Therefore, developing a "habit which looks upon the internal" seems a worthy goal for all new teachers. It is an appropriate first milestone—mark it on the map with a bright-colored pin—for the journey of learning to teach science in diverse classrooms.

Notes

Chapter 1

1. All names of institutions and individuals in this book are pseudonyms. University course titles, programs, and place names have also been altered to preserve anonymity.

2. Of the 55 secondary science student teachers in the four programs I studied, only four individuals did not identify as White. Census and school staffing data for the year of this study indicate that 90% of the people in the state identified as White, as did 93% of teachers.

3. Of particular value were studies by Bianchini and Cavazos (2007); Bianchini, Cavazos, and Rivas (2003); Brand and Glasson (2004); Cornbleth (2008); Luft, Bragg, and Peters (1999); and Rodriguez and Berryman (2002).

4. These were mainly tools from the Teacher Education and Learning to Teach (TELT) study (Kennedy, Ball, & McDiarmid, 1993; NCRTE, 1991) and the Educating Prospective Teachers of Biology study (Hewson, Tabachnick, Zeichner, Blomker, et al., 1999).

5. I collected data from participant interviews and questionnaires (pre-, mid-, and post-), teaching portfolios, written coursework and lesson-planning materials (shared via USB drives), and conducted multiple observations of participants' student teaching. Further information came from institutional teacher education program documents and interviews with university course instructors, program directors, and cooperating teachers. To get a better sense of how changes in participants' thinking connected back to their teacher preparation, I sat in on two semesters of Methods of Teaching Science courses at Briggstown University, where three of the participants (Armando, Jethro, and Kathy) were enrolled. My intent was to follow each of the participants for a year, although as will be shown, my time with Tyler and Armando was somewhat shorter.

Chapter 3

1. The actual interview question, which I call the "census question" in this book, was designed not only to elicit information about how they thought about

their own racial and ethnic identification but also to assess their overall thinking about how race and ethnicity operate in society. I showed all participants the
following question drawn from U.S. federal government guidelines for the collection of demographic information: "How would you describe yourself? (Circle
all that apply)." The choices included "American Indian or Alaska Native, Asian,
Black or African American, Hispanic or Latino, Native Hawaiian or Other Pa-
cific Islander, White," and "Other (please specify)." After they had been given
the opportunity to study the question, I asked participants to tell me what they
thought about when they saw this question or similar ones like it. I always found
their answers illuminating.

Chapter 4

1. During the year of this study, a shortage of science-certified cooperating
teachers at the district's middle school level led the SAMTEP program to adopt
a unique practicum design. One middle school teacher served as the cooperating teacher for 15 preservice science teachers, who were distributed across four
sections of her 6th-grade science students. She retained a fifth section at the end
of the day for herself. Over a period of 10 weeks, the SAMTEP students took
control of the planning and teaching of each class under the supervision of the
cooperating teacher. There were three to four practicum students in each class,
and during any given class period, one served as lead teacher. When not lead
teaching, practicum students acted as an instructional or classroom management
support; in some cases they simply observed class or operated video equipment.

Chapter 5

1. These are foundational concepts in the field of multicultural education
(Banks, 1995). *Content integration* concerns the use of content and examples
from cultures and groups to illustrate concepts in various subject areas. *Equity
pedagogy*, on the other hand, occurs when teachers teach in ways that facilitate
the academic achievement of students from diverse cultural, racial, socioeconomic, and gender groups. This may include adapting pedagogy to the cultural
characteristics and communication patterns of a particular group and making
sure that every student receives the attention and instruction they need to experience academic success.

Chapter 7

1. It is easy for the validity of educational research to be called into question when the subjects of the research are students of the researchers (e.g.,
Walsh, 2006), and the substance of such critique is not entirely groundless if

the researchers do not detail how relationships may have influenced findings. Therefore it is important to note that though I was Roberta's Methods of Teaching Science instructor during her second semester in the program, I was not her instructor for any other course. Once Roberta provided informed consent to participate in this study, she was not subject to my authority in any way. We did, however, have a professional history to our relationship, and this cannot be dismissed as irrelevant, either.

2. This phrasing is drawn from the work of Mica Pollock (2004).

References

AAA Executive Board. (1998). AAA statement on race. *American Anthropologist, 100*(3), 712–713.

Achinstein, B., & Aguirre, J. (2008). Cultural match or culturally suspect: How new teachers of color negotiate sociocultural challenges in the classroom. *Teachers College Record, 110*(8), 1505–1540.

Allport, G. W. (1979). *The nature of prejudice*. Reading, MA: Addison-Wesley

American Chemical Society. (1998). *ChemCom: Chemistry in the community* (3rd ed.). Dubuque, IA: Kendall/Hunt.

Anyon, J. (2005). *Radical possibilities: Public policy, urban education, and a new social movement*. New York: Routledge.

Apple, M. W. (1993). Constructing the "other": Rightist reconstructions of common sense. In C. McCarthy & W. Crichlow (Eds.), *Race, identity, and representation in education* (pp. 24–39). New York: Routledge.

Apple, M. W. (2000). *Official knowledge: Democratic education in a conservative age* (2nd ed.). New York: Routledge.

Atkin, J. M. (2005). *Designing everyday assessment in the science classroom*. New York: Teachers College Press.

Ball, D. L., Thames, M. H., & Phelps, G. (2008). Content knowledge for teaching: What makes it special? *Journal of Teacher Education, 59*(5), 389–407.

Banks, J. A. (1995). Multicultural education: Historical development, dimensions, and practice. In J. A. Banks & C. A. M. Banks (Eds.), *Handbook of research on multicultural education* (pp. 3–24). New York: Macmillan.

Barton, A. C. (2003). *Teaching science for social justice*. New York: Teachers College Press.

Bell, B., & Gilbert, J. (1996). *Teacher development: A model from science education*. London, UK: Falmer Press.

Berkman, M. B., Pacheco, J. S., & Plutzer, E. (2008). Evolution and creationism in America's classrooms: A national portrait. *PLOS Biology, 6*(5), e124. doi: 10.1371/journal.pbio.0060124

Berkman, M. B., & Plutzer, E. (2011). Defeating creationism in the courtroom, but not in the classroom. *Science, 331*(6016), 404–405. doi: 10.1126/science.1198902

Bianchini, J. A., & Cavazos, L. M. (2007). Learning from students, inquiry into practice, and participation in professional communities: Beginning teachers' uneven progress toward equitable science teaching. *Journal of Research in Science Teaching, 44*(4), 586–612.

Bianchini, J. A., Cavazos, L. M., & Rivas, M. (2003). At the intersection of contemporary descriptions of science and issues of equity and diversity: Student teachers' conceptions, rationales, and instructional practices. *Journal of Science Teacher Education, 14*(4), 259–290.

Black, P., & Wiliam, D. (1998). Inside the black box: Raising standards through classroom assessment. *Phi Delta Kappan, 80*(2), 139–148.

Boyd, D. J., Grossman, P., Lankford, H., Loeb, S., Michelli, N. M., & Wyckoff, J. (2006). Complex by design: Investigating pathways into teaching in New York city schools. *Journal of Teacher Education, 57*(2), 155–166. doi: 10.1177/0022487105285943

Brand, B. R., & Glasson, G. E. (2004). Crossing cultural borders into science teaching: Early life experiences, racial and ethnic identities, and beliefs about diversity. *Journal of Research in Science Teaching, 41*(2), 119–141.

Bransford, J. D., Brown, A. L., & Cocking, R. R. (Eds.). (1999). *How people learn: Brain, mind, experience, and school.* Washington, DC: National Academy Press.

Britzman, D. P. (2003). *Practice makes practice: A critical study of learning to teach* (Rev. ed.). Albany, NY: State University of New York Press.

Brown, B. A., & Spang, E. (2008). Double talk: Synthesizing everyday and science language in the classroom. *Science Education, 92*(4), 708–732.

Bybee, R. W. (1997). *Achieving scientific literacy: From purposes to practices.* Portsmouth, NH: Heinemann.

Calabrese Barton, A. (1998). *Feminist science education.* New York: Teachers College Press.

Chubbuck, S. M. (2004). Whiteness enacted, whiteness disrupted: The complexity of personal congruence. *American Educational Research Journal, 41*(2), 301–333.

Cochran-Smith, M. (2000). Blind vision. *Harvard Educational Review, 70*(2), 151–190.

Cochran-Smith, M., & Lytle, S. L. (2009). *Inquiry as stance: Practitioner research for the next generation.* New York: Teachers College Press.

Collins, H. M., & Pinch, T. J. (1998). *The golem: What you should know about science* (2nd ed.). New York: Cambridge University Press.

Compton-Lilly, C. (2003). *Reading families: The literate lives of urban children.* New York: Teachers College Press.

Conant, J. B. (1951). *Science and common sense.* New Haven, CT: Yale University Press.

Cornbleth, C. (2008). *Diversity and the new teacher: Learning from experience in urban schools.* New York: Teachers College Press.

Darling-Hammond, L. (2006). *Powerful teacher education: Lessons from exemplary programs.* San Francisco: Jossey-Bass.

Darling-Hammond, L., Baratz-Snowden, J. C., & National Academy of Education (Eds.). (2005). *A good teacher in every classroom: Preparing the highly qualified teachers our children deserve.* San Francisco: Jossey-Bass.

Davis, E. A., Petish, D., & Smithey, J. (2006). Challenges new science teachers face. *Review of Educational Research, 76*(4), 607–651.

Delpit, L. D. (1988). The silenced dialogue: Power and pedagogy in educating other people's children. *Harvard Educational Review, 58*(3), 280–298.

Delpit, L. D. (2002). No kinda sense. In L. D. Delpit & J. K. Dowdy (Eds.), *The skin that we speak: Thoughts on language and culture in the classroom* (pp. 31–48). New York: The New York Press.

Dennett, D. C. (2003). *Freedom evolves.* New York: Penguin Books.

Dewey, J. (1904/2008). The relation of theory to practice in education. In M. Cochran-Smith, S. Feiman-Nemser, D. J. McIntyre, & Association of Teacher Educators (Eds.), *Handbook of research on teacher education: Enduring questions in changing contexts* (3rd ed., pp. 787–799). New York: Routledge.

Dilworth, M. E., & Brown, A. L. (2008). Teachers of color: Quality and effective teachers one way or another. In M. Cochran-Smith, S. Feiman-Nemser, D. J. McIntyre, & Association of Teacher Educators. (Eds.), *Handbook of research on teacher education: Enduring questions in changing contexts* (3rd ed.) pp. 424–444). New York: Routledge.

Duckworth, E. R. (2006). *"The having of wonderful ideas" and other essays on teaching and learning* (3rd ed.). New York: Teachers College Press.

Duschl, R. A., & Grandy, R. E. (2008). Reconsidering the character and role of inquiry in school science: Framing the debates. In R. A. Duschl & R. E. Grandy (Eds.), *Teaching scientific inquiry* (pp. 1-37). Rotterdam, Netherlands: Sense Publishers.

Edmonds, L. (2009). Challenges and solutions for ELLs. *The Science Teacher, 76*(3), 30–33.

Freire, P. (1970). *Pedagogy of the oppressed.* New York: Herder and Herder.

Fuller, F. F. (1969). Concerns of teachers: A developmental conceptualization. *American Educational Research Journal, 6*(2).

Gamoran, A. (1992). Access to excellence: Assignment to honors English classes in the transition from middle to high school. *Educational Evaluation and Policy Analysis, 14*(3), 185–204.

Gay, G. (2002). Preparing for culturally responsive teaching. *Journal of Teacher Education, 53*(2), 106–116.

Glasser, W. (1990). *The quality school: Managing students without coercion.* New York: Perennial Library.

Gollnick, D. M. (2008). Teacher capacity for diversity. In M. Cochran-Smith, S. Feiman-Nemser, D. J. McIntyre, & Association of Teacher Educators (Eds.), *Handbook of research on teacher education: Enduring questions in changing contexts* (3rd ed.) pp. 249–257. New York: Routledge.

Gomez, M. L., Walker, A. B., & Page, M. L. (2000). Personal experience as a guide to teaching. *Teaching and Teacher Education, 16*(7), 731.

González, N., Moll, L. C., & Amanti, C. (2005). *Funds of knowledge: Theorizing practices in households, communities, and classrooms.* Mahwah, NJ: Lawrence Erlbaum Associates.

Gorski, P. (2006). The classist underpinnings of Ruby Payne's framework. *Teachers College Record.* Available at http://www.tcrecord.org/content.asp?contentid=12322

Grant, C. A., & Agosto, V. (2006). What are we tripping on?: Trangressing the fault lines in research on the preparation of multicultural educators. In C. Conrad & R. C. Serlin (Eds.), *The Sage handbook for research in education: Engaging ideas and enriching inquiry* (pp. 95–115). Thousand Oaks, CA: Sage Publications.

Grant, C. A., & Secada, W. (1990). Preparing teachers for diversity. In W. R. Houston, M. Haberman, & J. P. Sikula (Eds.), *Handbook of research on teacher education: A project of the association of teacher educators* (pp. 403–422). New York: Collier Macmillan.

Grant, C. A., & Sleeter, C. E. (2003). *Turning on learning: Five approaches for multicultural teaching plans for race, class, gender, and disability* (3rd ed.). New York: John Wiley & Sons.

Grant, C. A., & Sleeter, C. E. (2007). *Doing multicultural education for achievement and equity*. New York: Routledge.

Haberman, M. (1991). The pedagogy of poverty versus good teaching. *Phi Delta Kappan, 73*(4), 290–294.

Haberman, M. (2007, July). *The source and nature of best practice in teaching*. Paper presented at the Association of Teacher Educators Summer Conference, Milwaukee, WI.

Hammerness, K., Darling-Hammond, L., Bransford, J., Berliner, D., Cochran-Smith, M., McDonald, M., & Zeichner, K. M. (2005). How teachers learn and develop. In L. Darling-Hammond & J. Bransford (Eds.), *Preparing teachers for a changing world: What teachers should learn and be able to do* (1st ed., pp. 358–389). San Francisco, CA: Jossey-Bass.

Handal, G., & Lauvas, P. (1987). *Promoting reflective teaching: Supervision in practice*. Buckinghamshire, UK: Milton Keynes, Society for Research into Higher Education & Open University Press.

Hattie, J., & Timperley, H. (2007). The power of feedback. *Review of Educational Research, 77*(1), 81–112.

Heath, S. B. (1983). *Ways with words : Language, life, and work in communities and classrooms*. New York: Cambridge University Press.

Hestenes, D., Wells, M., & Swackhamer, G. (1992). Force concept inventory. *The Physics Teacher, 30*, 141–158.

Hewitt, P. G. (1992). *Conceptual physics: The high school physics program* (2nd ed.). Menlo Park, CA: Addison-Wesley Publishing Company.

Hewitt, P. G. (2011). Equations as guides to thinking and problem solving. *The Physics Teacher, 49*(5). doi: 10.1119/1.3578413

Hewson, P. W. (1985). Epistemological commitments in the learning of science: Examples from dynamics. *European Journal of Science Education, 7*(2), 163–172.

Hewson, P. W. (1992, June). *Conceptual change in science teaching and teacher education*. Paper presented at the meeting on "Research and Curriculum Development in Science Teaching," National Center for Educational Research, Documentation, and Assessment, Ministry for Education and Science, Madrid, Spain. Available at http://www.learner.org/channel/workshops/lala2/support/hewson.pdf

Hewson, P. W., & Lemberger, J. (2000). Status as the hallmark of conceptual learning. In R. Millar, J. Leach & J. Osborne (Eds.), *Improving science education: The contribution of research* (pp. 110–125). Buckingham, UK: Open University Press.

Hewson, P. W., Tabachnick, B. R., Zeichner, K. M., Blomker, K. B., Meyer, H., Lemberger, J., Marion, R., Park, H., & Toolin, R. (1999). Educating prospective teachers of biology: Introduction and research methods. *Science Education, 83*(3), 247–273.

Hewson, P. W., Tabachnick, B. R., Zeichner, K. M., & Lemberger, J. (1999). Educating prospective teachers of biology: Findings, limitations, and recommendations. *Science Education, 83*(3), 373–384.

Howes, E. V. (2002). *Connecting girls and science: Constructivism, feminism, and science education reform.* New York: Teachers College Press.

Iceland, J., Weinberg, D. H., Steinmetz, E., & United States Bureau of the Census. (2002). *Racial and ethnic residential segregation in the United States 1980–2000.* Washington, DC: U.S. Census Bureau.

Jablonski, N. G. (2006). *Skin: A natural history.* Berkeley: University of California Press.

Jaspin, E. (2007). *Buried in the bitter waters: The hidden history of racial cleansing in America.* New York: Basic Books.

Kahneman, D. (2011). *Thinking, fast and slow* (1st ed.). New York: Farrar, Straus and Giroux.

Kennedy, M. M. (1998). *Learning to teach writing: Does teacher education make a difference?* New York: Teachers College Press.

Kennedy, M. M., Ball, D. L., & McDiarmid, G. W. (1993). A study package for examining and tracking changes in teachers' knowledge. NCTRL technical series 93-1. Available at http://ncrtl.msu.edu/http/tseries/ts931.htm

Key, S. G. (2003). Enhancing the science interest of African American students using cultural inclusion. In S. M. Hines (Ed.), *Multicultural science education: Theory, practice, and promise* (pp. 87–101). New York: Peter Lang.

King, J. E. (1991). Dysconcious racism: Ideology, identity, and the miseducation of teachers. *Journal of Negro Education, 60*(2), 133–146.

Kohn, A. (1993). *Punished by rewards: The trouble with gold stars, incentive plans, A's, praise, and other bribes.* Boston: Houghton Mifflin.

Kozol, J. (1991). *Savage inequalities: Children in America's schools* (1st ed.). New York: Crown Publishers.

Kozol, J. (2005). *The shame of the nation: The restoration of apartheid schooling in America.* New York: Crown Publishers.

Kozol, J. (2007). *Letters to a young teacher.* New York: Crown Publishers.

Kuhn, T. S. (1970). *The structure of scientific revolutions* (2nd ed.). Chicago: University of Chicago Press.

Ladson-Billings, G. (1994). *The dreamkeepers: Successful teachers of African American children* (1st ed.). San Francisco: Jossey-Bass.

Ladson-Billings, G. (1999). Preparing teachers for diverse student populations: A critical race theory perspective. *Review of research in education* (Vol. 24, pp. 211–247).

Ladson-Billings, G. (2000). Racialized discourses and ethnic epistemologies. In N. Denzin & Y. Lincoln (Eds.), *Handbook of qualitative research* (2nd ed.). Thousand Oaks, CA: Sage.

Ladson-Billings, G. (2006). It's not the culture of poverty, it's the poverty of culture: The problem with teacher education. *Anthropology and Education Quarterly, 37*(2), 104.

Lakoff, G., & Johnson, M. (1980). *Metaphors we live by*. Chicago: University of Chicago Press.

Lee, C. D. (2007). *Culture, literacy, and learning: Taking bloom in the midst of the whirlwind*. New York: Teachers College Press.

Lomawaima, K. T. (1995). Educating Native Americans. In J. A. Banks & C. A. M. Banks (Eds.), *Handbook of research on multicultural education* (pp. 331–347). New York: Macmillan.

Longstreet, W. S. (1997). Ethnic studies. In C. A. Grant & G. Ladson-Billings (Eds.), *Dictionary of multicultural education*. Phoenix, AZ: Oryx Press.

Louv, R. (2005). *Last child in the woods: Saving our children from nature-deficit disorder* (1st ed.). Chapel Hill, NC: Algonquin Books of Chapel Hill.

Luft, J. A., Bragg, J., & Peters, C. (1999). Learning to teach in a diverse setting: A case study of a multicultural science education enthusiast. *Science Education, 83*(5), 527–544.

Mitakidou, S., Tressou, E., Swadener, B. B., & Grant, C. A. (2009). *Beyond pedagogies of exclusion: Transnational conversations*. New York: Palgrave MacMillan.

National Research Council. (1996). *National science education standards*. Washington, DC: National Academy Press.

National Research Council. (2007). Taking science to school: Learning and teaching science in grades K-8. In R. A. Duschl, H. A. Schweingruber, A. W. Shouse, & Committee on Science Learning Kindergarten Through Eighth Grade. (Eds.). Washington, DC: National Academies Press.

National Research Council. (2012). *A framework for K–12 science education: Practices, crosscutting concepts, and core ideas*. Washington, DC: The National Academies Press.

NCRTE. (1991). Findings from the teacher education and learning to teach study: Final report. Available at http://ncrtl.msu.edu/http/sreports/sr691.pdf

Nickerson, R. S. (2004). *Cognition and chance: The psychology of probabilistic reasoning*. Mahwah, NJ: Lawrence Erlbaum Associates.

Oakes, J. (2005). *Keeping track: How schools structure inequality* (2nd ed.). New Haven, CT: Yale University Press.

Paine, L. (1990). *Orientations towards diversity: What do prospective teachers bring?* (Research Report 89-9). East Lansing, MI: Michigan State University, National Center for Research on Teacher Learning.

Paley, V. G. (1989). *White teacher*. Cambridge, MA: Harvard University Press.

Payne, R. K. (2005). *A framework for understanding poverty* (2nd ed.). Highlands, TX: aha! Process, Inc.

Pintrich, P. R., Marx, R. W., & Boyle, R. A. (1993). Beyond cold conceptual change: The role of motivational beliefs and classroom contextual factors in the process of conceptual change. *Review of Educational Research, 63*(2), 167–199.

Pollock, M. (2004). *Colormute: Race talk dilemmas in an American school.* Princeton, NJ: Princeton University Press.

Posner, G. J., Strike, K. A., Hewson, P. W., & Gertzog, W. A. (1982). Accommodation of a scientific conception: Toward a theory of conceptual change. *Science Education, 66*(2), 211–227.

Rodriguez, A. J. (1998). Strategies for counterresistance: Toward sociotransformative constructivism and learning to teach science for diversity and for understanding. *Journal of Research in Science Teaching, 35*(6), 589–622.

Rodriguez, A. J., & Berryman, C. (2002). Using sociotransformative constructivism to teach for understanding in diverse classrooms: A beginning teacher's journey *American Educational Research Journal, 39*(4), 1017–1035.

Roth, W. M., & Lee, S. (2002). Scientific literacy as collective praxis. *Public Understanding of Science, 11*(1), 33–56.

Rudolph, J. L. (2007). An inconvenient truth about science education. *Teachers College Record, February 09, 2007.* Available at http://www.tcrecord.org/content. asp?contentid=13216

Russell, T., & Martin, A. K. (2007). Learning to teach science. In S. K. Abell & N. G. Lederman (Eds.), *Handbook of research on science education* (pp. 1151–1178). Mahwah, NJ: Lawrence Erlbaum Associates.

Sato, M., & Lensmire, T. J. (2009). Poverty and Payne: Supporting teachers to work with children of poverty. *Phi Delta Kappan, 90*(5), 365–370.

Shulman, L. S. (1986). Those who understand: Knowledge growth in teaching. *Educational Researcher, 15*(2), 4–14.

Shulman, L. S. (1987). Knowledge and teaching: Foundations of the new reform. *Harvard Educational Review, 57*(1), 1–22.

Sleeter, C. E. (2001). Preparing teachers for culturally diverse schools: Research and the overwhelming presence of whiteness. *Journal of Teacher Education, 52*(2), 94–106.

Smith, C. L., Maclin, D., Houghton, C., & Hennessey, M. G. (2000). Sixth-grade students' epistemologies of science: The impact of school science experiences on epistemological development. *Cognition and Instruction, 18*(3), 349–422.

Smith, L. T. (1999). *Decolonizing methodologies: Research and indigenous peoples.* New York: St. Martin's Press.

Spady, W. G. (1994). *Outcome-based education: Critical issues and answers.* Arlington, VA: American Association of School Administrators.

Spindler, G. D., & Spindler, L. S. (1990). *The American cultural dialogue and its transmission.* New York: Falmer Press.

Steele, C. (2010). *Whistling Vivaldi: And other clues to how stereotypes affect us* (1st ed.). New York: W.W. Norton & Company.

Taleb, N. (2007). *The black swan: The impact of the highly improbable* (1st ed.). New York: Random House.

Tatum, B. D. (2003). *"Why are all the black kids sitting together in the cafeteria?" And other conversations about race.* New York: Basic Books.

Thompson, G. L. (2004). *Through ebony eyes: What teachers need to know but are afraid to ask about African American students.* San Francisco, CA: Jossey-Bass.

Thompson, J., Braaten, M., & Windschitl, M. (2009). *Learning progression as vision tools for advancing novice teachers' pedagogical performance.* Paper presented at the Learning Progressions in Science (LeaPS) conference, Iowa City.

Toulmin, S. E. (1972). *Human understanding.* Princeton, NJ: Princeton University Press.

Tucker, M. (1998, September 1). Multiculturalism's five dimensions: An interview with James Banks. *NEA Today.*

Tyson, N. d. (2007). *Death by black hole and other cosmic quandaries* (1st ed.). New York: W.W. Norton.

U.S. Census Bureau. (1997). Recommendations from the interagency committee for the review of the racial and ethnic standards to the Office of Management and Budget concerning changes to the standards for the classification of federal data on race and ethnicity. Washington, DC. Available at http://www.census.gov/population/www/socdemo/race/Directive_15.html.

U.S. Commission on Civil Rights. (2006). Racial categorization in the 2010 census. A briefing before the United States Commission on Civil Rights held in Washington, DC, April 7, 2006. Available at http://www.usccr.gov/pubs/RC2010Web_Version.pdf

Valli, L. (1995). The dilemma of race: Learning to be color blind and color conscious. *Journal of Teacher Education, 46*(2), 120–129.

Villegas, A. M. (2007). Dispositions in teacher education: A look at social justice. *Journal of Teacher Education, 58*(5), 370–380.

Villegas, A. M., & Davis, D. (2008). Preparing teachers of color to confront racial/ethnic disparities in educational outcomes. In M. Cochran-Smith, S. Feiman-Nemser, D. J. McIntyre & Association of Teacher Educators. (Eds.), *Handbook of research on teacher education: Enduring questions in changing contexts* (3rd ed.) pp. 583–605. New York: Routledge; Co-published by the Association of Teacher Educators.

Villegas, A. M., & Lucas, T. (2002). Preparing culturally responsive teachers: Rethinking the curriculum. *Journal of Teacher Education, 53*(1), 20–32.

Walsh, K. (2006). Teacher education: Coming up empty. Washington, DC. Available at http://www.nctq.org/p/publications/docs/Teacher_Education_fwd_20080316034429.pdf

Warren, B., Ballenger, C., Ogonowski, M., Rosebery, A. S., Hudicourt-Barnes, J. (2001). Rethinking diversity in learning science: The logic of everyday sense-making. *Journal of Research in Science Teaching, 38*(5), 529–552.

Windschitl, M. (2004). Folk theories of "inquiry": How preservice teachers reproduce the discourse and practices of an atheoretical scientific method. *Journal of Research in Science Teaching, 41*(5), 481–512.

Windschitl, M., & Thompson, J. (2006). Transcending simple forms of school science investigation: The impact of preservice instruction on teachers' understandings of model-based inquiry. *American Educational Research Journal, 43*(4), 783–835.

Zeichner, K. (1996). Educating teachers for cultural diversity. In K. M. Zeichner, S. L. Melnick, & M. L. Gomez (Eds.), *Currents of reform in preservice teacher education* (pp. 133–175). New York: Teachers College Press.

Zeichner, K. (2009). *Teacher education and the struggle for social justice.* New York: Routledge.

Index

149

EDUCATION LIBRARY
UNIVERSITY OF KENTUCKY

About the Author

Douglas B. Larkin is an assistant professor in the Department of Secondary and Special Education at Montclair State University in Montclair, New Jersey. He worked as a high school physics and chemistry teacher for ten years and served as a U.S. Peace Corps volunteer in Kenya and Papua New Guinea. He received his PhD in Teacher Education from the University of Wisconsin–Madison. His research concerns the preparation of science teachers for culturally diverse classrooms. He currently works with preservice secondary science and math teachers in the Newark-Montclair Urban Teacher Residency Program and teaches in the teacher education and teacher development doctoral program.